ASHE

Also in Lion's Roar

ADHISHTHANA: THE VIEW AND PRACTICE OF NGÖNDRO

ASHE

& the Four Dignities

THE KONGMA SAKYONG,
JAMPAL TRINLEY DRADÜL

Compiled and edited by Emily Hilburn Sell

LION'S ROAR
HALIFAX & COLOGNE
2009

Access to this publication is restricted to students who have received lungta and stroke transmission.

Lion's Roar
An imprint of Shambhala Media
3008 Oxford St., Suite 201
Halifax, NS B3L 2W5
902-421-1550
orders@shambhalashop.com
www.shambhalashop.com

ISBN 978-1-55055-051-1

First Edition
10 9 8 7 6 5 4 3 2 1

Printed in Canada

CONTENTS

IV ACTING OUT REALITY

HRIH

The virtuous mark, the great banner of inspiring windhorse,
And these clouds of offerings of all desirable things
We offer to you, great being Gesar with your retinue.
Fulfill all our wishes; be victorious in all directions.

I
THE VISION OF ASHE

1
Awakening Confidence with Ashe

THE SHAMBHALA TERMA

One of the most important teachings we have, a unique teaching that is ours alone, is the teaching on Ashe and windhorse. After meditating, studying, and deepening our practice with insight, we receive these profoundly practical teachings.

My father Chögyam Trungpa Rinpoche, the Dorje Dradül of Mukpo, was a seminal influence in bringing Buddhism to the West. These teachings on Ashe and windhorse are part of one of the Dorje Dradül's most profound contributions—the Shambhala *terma*, which were first revealed to him when he was a teenager in Tibet. Whereas *kama* teachings have been handed down directly from teacher to student since the time of Shakyamuni Buddha, terma teachings are hidden for a period of time, revealed only at the particular time and place that they are most helpful, most needed.

When asked about the sources of the Shambhala texts, the

Dorje Dradül replied, "the Rigden fathers and Mr. Gesar." He further explained that Gesar of Ling is a manifestation of Padmasambhava and the vanguard of the Shambhala teachings. Therefore, there is a deep-rooted connection between the terma revealed by the Dorje Dradül as the Shambhala teachings and the tradition of Buddhism in Tibet. In fact, they are inseparable from the Buddhist teachings.

The Shambhala terma were brought to the Dorje Dradül by visions of *werma* and *drala*. The word *drala* literally means "above the enemy." Werma is a gathering of enlightened drala, which is the unconditioned wisdom and power of the world that exists simply in things as they are, beyond duality or aggression.

Specifically, these visions came from the Rigdens and from Shiwa Ökar, whose name means "Peaceful White Light." Often Shiwa Ökar is referred to as the *lha* of lha—the divine of the divine—the ultimate principle of the most primordial reality, which we call primordial Ashe, or the confidence of all. The Rigdens are the manifestation of the energy, brilliance, and wisdom of that completely enlightened space. Drala and werma like the Rigdens and Shiwa Ökar are none other than the innate wisdom and mercy of our own mind, which we call Great Eastern Sun.

The Dorje Dradül wrote everything down from these visions, but the texts were lost during his escape from Tibet to India. Then over the course of time they were re-revealed to him. His Holiness Dilgo Khyentse Rinpoche confirmed them as terma. Later the teachings became what is now Shambhala

Training. Through Shambhala Training they have manifested in an almost worldly way, so we don't always keep in mind how precious they are. However, when we asked Khyentse Rinpoche what to do if other important lamas were to request them, his answer was surprising: "First they need to do the Shambhala training, because these are very, very important teachings."

What we consider the Shambhala lineage is unique and vast, stemming from the many traditions that the Dorje Dradül himself held and practiced, as well as those he initiated. The Dorje Dradül's intention was for Shambhala—especially the terma that he revealed—to be the basis of our view, practice, and meditation. He often talked about Shambhala as the container of the Buddhist teachings, as the mountain that supports and protects them.

The Shambhala teachings present a world that we do not abandon, but rather, engage in. We understand the vicissitudes of suffering while trying to nurture our inherent basic goodness and the Ashe, the confidence of all. These teachings encourage us not to have our private stash of spirituality hidden away. They say that a genuine spiritual practice is having no privacy and laying down our life and mind for the welfare of others. This is what we call enlightened society, enlightened world, or the kingdom of Shambhala. If this occurs, then, as it says in the text, "a new golden age dawns." The golden age is the opposite of the setting sun, *samsara*, in which—just like at dusk—there is not much daylight left and we are distracted by entertainment, idleness, and laziness.

Having received these teachings, we are called to arms to wake up and fly the Shambhala banner high. This is the notion of Great East. We must have confidence in our goodness, which is windhorse, or *lungta*. We must abandon negativity by cultivating virtue and *wangthang*, authentic presence. Then we have glory, *ziji*.

Instructions on how to magnetize and raise confidence are found in other teachings, especially in the works of Jamgön Mipham Rinpoche, the prolific nineteenth-century luminary who wrote extensively about Shambhala, drala, and werma. So in terms of the historical context, the Dorje Dradül was not pulling these teachings from thin air, but drawing on ancestry that dates back to ancient Central and South Asia. He had visions inspired by Padmasambhava, Gesar, and the Rigdens; he was also drawing on his own upbringing in Tibet and the teachings he received based on the principles of Shambhala.

The Rigden kings of Shambhala are themselves, in fact, *bodhisattvas*. We invoke them as guardians because they have taken a vow to protect sentient beings. In particular we invoke them because we are trying to create and establish a society based on the notion that the human mind and heart are pure from beginningless time, and that we can develop that view. We are trying to create a society where people can live in harmony and draw from the powers of basic goodness, the unconditional purity and confidence of all.

THE ESSENCE OF SHAMBHALA

The Shambhala seal has a garuda holding the four dignities—tiger, lion, garuda, and dragon—with the Tibetan
words *sab sel song tsen küntu gyal* underneath. That means
"profound, brilliant, just, powerful, all-victorious." The
phrase "profound, brilliant, just, powerful, all-victorious"
describes the innate goodness of all beings. It is profound, it
is vast, it is just.

Profound, brilliant, just, powerful, and all-victorious are
general terms; it's hard to know exactly what they mean. We
have to deepen our understanding by contemplating and
studying them. But we need an image to which we can attach
our understanding. What does it mean to have wisdom, to be
compassionate, to have conviction, to have life-force energy?
As our understanding of these questions increases, we bring it
to the Ashe.

In tantric Buddhist practices we have something called a
soy-yik, seed syllable. *Soy* means "essence," "main," and *yik*
means "letter" or "symbolism." One of the most common seed
syllables is the seed syllable HUM, which occurs in the *Sadhana
of Mahamudra*. HUM represents the energies of all five buddha
families. For the Shambhala terma, the soy-yik, the essence, is
the Ashe. When we say "Ashe," we are talking about the most
primordial, basic essence of what things are.

The teachings on lungta and Ashe instruct us in how to access basic goodness. The Ashe itself represents the primordial
innate confidence that all beings possess. It is the complete
confidence of egolessness, the potent ability to recognize the

nature of reality. When we visualize the Ashe, we engender a level of relative confidence, the element of genuineness. The Dorje Dradül has passed along his visions about how we can access these qualities and bring them about.

Ultimately, at the basis, the mind is fundamentally good. "Good" means that there is an opportunity to take the mind beyond the distortion and torment of emotions. We can actually live a life where we are not continuously aggravated by negativity, discursiveness, or misunderstandings about the nature of things, which are the barbarians we talk about. In Shambhala, our fundamental objective is to take a hopeful approach toward the future—and the present—in terms of developing this opportunity.

ZIJI

In lungta practice we visualize the Ashe descending into our heart center. There it awakens or shocks our innate ziji. Ziji—"glorious, shining"—describes the kind of confidence that comes from realizing basic goodness. Even on a mundane level, when we want to accomplish something, we need our ziji, our potency. We need to drink our glass of Ziji in the morning. We can use it as a brand name here. Ziji is the quality that I see in people who are doing Shambhala training, in people who are doing a retreat, and it is also the result of those situations. They look as if they can do whatever they want.

Ziji means that because the warrior is awake and confident, he or she manifests as brilliant and magnetizing. We're drawn to someone who manifests this state of mind, which is completely absorbed and maturated in basic goodness and the noble qualities, *yönten.*

Ziji is the result of "the complete gathering of all perfect things." What are perfect things? On a relative level, they are long life, health, and wealth—all these elements everybody is trying to achieve. In addition ziji includes our inherent, enlightened qualities—compassion, wisdom, and insight. This perfect gathering comes from realizing the confidence of Ashe. That's why the text calls Ashe "the *A* of life."

ASHE, PRAJNA, AND THE GREAT EASTERN SUN

Raising windhorse through the practice of Ashe sharpens our *prajna,* "best knowledge." What are the best things to know? Wisdom is the best thing to know. The ground nature is the best thing to know. With prajna we see things as they really are. When we know how things are, we no longer feel fear. The warrior therefore behaves in a fearless way.

What is the seed of fearlessness? Not being confused by our own mind. When we aren't confused by our own mind, we're not afraid of it either, and we're able to see what is going on in the minds and hearts of others. The result is benevolence and kindness. Because we are no longer afraid, we can begin to lead others in a kind, benevolent way.

It is important to understand what these words mean in different contexts. We may ask, "Is benevolence like compassion?" Of course it has compassion in it. Benevolence is also rooted in patience, which results in gentleness, absence of aggression. Our mind becomes spacious and our innate compassion is able to blossom.

The Shambhala tradition draws on the principles of the warrior, who is not a recluse cowering from the burdens of the world, but one who engages in it wholeheartedly. We humans do not have to be embarrassed about who we are. We do not have to try to protect ourselves from the intensity of the world's suffering. Appreciating certain truths about existence allows us to live our lives with fearlessness. We discover a sense of our destiny, as opposed to giving in to a defeatist mind.

As warriors we engage the world in an unconventional way because we give up gain, and thus we give up loss. We give up victory, fame, and any idea of trying to accomplish something through those means. By practicing the four kinds of confidence—tiger, lion, garuda, and dragon—we begin to understand the nature of our being. We become less confused about the nature of phenomena.

Once we begin to understand the nature of phenomena beyond gain and loss, we glimpse the purity and equality of all things. We have foresight; we see what is going on in the bigger picture, because we sense the vastness of the Great Eastern Sun, *sharchen nyima*. "Great" means that this wisdom is all-pervasive. "East" means it is perpetual, always available. "Sun" means that it illuminates everything, just like the physical sun. Without this kind of wisdom, we live in the dark age, not knowing what is happening.

The Great Eastern Sun and the four dignities are infused

in the image and practice of Ashe. The practices of stroke and raising windhorse are tangible ways to rouse them. We can also raise lungta in our environment with mundane activities such as cleaning our space, wearing nice clothes, spending time with people who increase our energy, eating decent food, or walking in nature to understand where the energy or drala is. These are ways we cultivate an external view of how to raise lungta. We can also perform various ceremonies. But here we're talking about internally raising that energy.

If we place the mind we have right now in a confident, precise, and accurate way, at this very moment we can see the original unobstructed purity that has been there since the beginning of time and continues to happen. This allows us to be more settled and have conviction in the purpose of our life. It allows us to be genuine. That is the magic of the practice of Ashe.

2

WISDOM FOR A DARK AGE

A GREAT BODHISATTVA like the Dorje Dradül understands how best to infuse any particular environment with the essence of the teachings. This is a dark age. When he received the Shambhala teachings, he saw that in order for the buddhadharma not to be overwhelmed by the darkness, the teachings of the Rigdens and of Gesar needed to come out.

What is a dark age? The Tibetan term literally means the residue time, what is left over, the dregs. What is left over are the remnants of *gewa* or virtue, positive actions. We are in an era when virtue is on the wane. The negative, turbulent, nonvirtuous qualities of human existence—the barbarians—are overcoming compassion and wakefulness—the elements that move us forward in our development. Our perceptions are sludgy and dull. We don't appreciate who we are or what we have. We are confused about what is important, so we are mean to ourselves and to each other. There is little opportunity to practice.

Dark age—what the Shambhala teachings call "setting sun"—affects us on many levels. The darkness is related with our personal life-force energy; what is setting is our ability to experience basic goodness. The more that goes down, the heavier the mind becomes. That is the notion of darkness: it is heavy and it obscures our ground nature. The darkest of the dark ages needs the most profound and powerful teaching because our aggression and lack of compassion are very thick and intense. When we are motivated by *klesha*—strong negative emotions like greed and anger—our windhorse diminishes and we act barbarically.

On an outer level, barbarians are those who kill or cause harm. The inner barbarians are kleshas such as anger and jealousy. At the secret level, the barbarian is our mind holding onto the dualistic concept of seeing ourselves as solid and the world as ordinary. Not understanding basic goodness, we begin to see the world as separate from our own mind. Our projections cause fear and concept. The result is a sense of nonpossibility, cowardice in a very small way—not rising to the occasion. Compassion seems trite. Being nice, or contemplating the Shambhala principles, seems like too much effort. This is the life force sinking in us. The result of barbaric activity—whether it's in the form of weapons, wrong motivation, or holding onto concept—is that we feel pain.

In this time we're living in, there is heightened materialism, not just because there are more computers and cars, but because there is a heightened assault on the mind. There is more speed, more information, and the mind has to hold more and more in order to get its orientation. This reduces the life-force energy.

A DIRECT COMMUNICATION

In this particular time, it is essential to stabilize and understand the nature of the mind. But it is not easy to become stable in our understanding of basic goodness. Knowing this, the great Dorje Dradül has given us the practice of Ashe, which is a wisdom method for stabilizing our understanding and sharpening our confidence. With this practice we gain the fearlessness that comes from experiencing our genuine mind.

In this particular dark time, we can't really *feel* properly because of our ego. Because of that ego-ness, we become numb, dumb, and thick. Nothing really touches us anymore. Even when we sit down and practice, we are often just maintaining our story line and habit with the addition of a little spirituality.

In offering these teachings, the Dorje Dradül is not some Martian looking down on us. He's living here, experiencing the ups and downs and pains. But he has a realized mind and he's trying to communicate to us how things really are. There will always be sadness and happiness, wisdom and ignorance, virtue and nonvirtue: all of it will perpetually go on. Through the practice of Ashe we can train in removing our focus from these illusory aspects and returning it to the natural state. Ashe draws down drala. The Shambhala tradition tells us that the dralas, war gods, are here to overcome obstacles.

When we're doing Ashe and windhorse practice, the more

we understand the Shambhala root texts, the deeper we'll be able to go. The Dorje Dradül is a master of the mahayana and vajrayana teachings. The Shambhala terma is his final statement on reality, his final realization, and there are no holds barred. He's saying that reality has no color, and therefore the primordial Ashe is colorless, and that all beings have the ability to have complete wisdom, the Great Eastern Sun.

It's important to realize that the Dorje Dradül very carefully chose certain words that directly transmit reality, translating them into English in particular ways. Each word is a profound transmission of its own particular truth. We might get into asking questions like, "Is basic goodness the same as buddha nature?" Of course we can correlate the meaning of these terms with the language of the Buddhist teachings: we can say that absolute Ashe is emptiness, or that the Great Eastern Sun is wisdom. But at the same time, we need to recognize that here is a great master who is presenting a certain teaching in a particular language for the benefit of those who are listening to it. We have a great teacher saying, "This is the way I am going to express what is taking place; this is the way that is beneficial for you."

The language of wisdom is actually beyond even using the word "wisdom." This is the light in which the Dorje Dradül proclaimed the Shambhala teachings, which are very advanced teachings, very high teachings. Through his own realization, he had a direct experience of reality and of the ultimate nature. He had a vision of Shiwa Ökar—the divine warrior being who transmitted to him—and from that he wrote these root texts and practices, which are communicating directly how we can become enlightened, not by abandoning the world or our senses, but by engaging in an enlightened way.

WHY WARRIORSHIP?

In this particular dark age, when we are constantly seeking pleasure or comfort, we have a tendency to become cowardly and lazy. In such a period we need more action-oriented practices and teachings. Therefore Shambhala lineage beings like Shiwa Ökar, the Rigdens, and Gesar manifest as warriors.

The genealogical lifeblood lineage of Gesar of Ling is the Mukpo clan. Where there is Mukpo, there is the protective quality of Gesar. According to the Dorje Dradül's brother, Damchö Rinpoche, after the Dorje Dradül began receiving the Shambhala terma on a retreat when he was about twelve years old, my father started using his family name of Mukpo. Damchö Rinpoche, who was with him on several retreats, told me that even though at that time the Dorje Dradül was a monk, the Rigdens commanded him to continue the Mukpo lineage in order to bring the activity of Gesar back into the world in this era of materialism and barbarians.

That is how we have become Shambhala warriors in this particular time of decreasing life force, which means that the potential for enlightenment and for creating enlightened society seem to be waning. From a meditative physiological point of view, we do have a life force, and it does begin to wane. Everything has a grayish hue. Obviously we are talking about a journey of the mind. One day we are in a hard, dark alley in a big city and we see reality as hard and dark. But the next day we are in a beautiful meadow, and all of a sudden "reality" looks very different.

Because the Great Eastern Sun shines from our mind and heart center, the golden dawn of Shambhala cannot be anywhere but here. If it were somewhere else, it would be objectified, physical; it would no longer have the Rigden quality. In that case we would have permanence, existence, which implies a beginning and an end.

MAKING A DEFINITE STROKE

For every conceptual thought, there is a teaching. For every moment in the day, there is a teaching. For every blade of grass, there is a teaching. For every emotion, there is a teaching. And what is the teaching? It is that even when we're in the throes of thick passion or sharp anger, it is possible to see the pure radiance of the Great Eastern Sun. In sleeping and in waking, this awareness cannot be destroyed. It is the crown jewel. In a dark age, this particular jewel becomes more difficult to obtain because our minds are continuously attacked and possessed by materialism—outer, inner, and secret. Outer materialism is imagining external phenomena to be real, inner materialism is imagining thoughts to be real, and secret materialism is the mind's habit of holding on. The result of holding on is aggression.

One characteristic of a dark age is that aggression has laid its hands all over every situation. At times this might feel overwhelming. We might say, "It is too much effort to raise windhorse, to invoke this kind of energy." We must be sensible about the whole thing. We have to be able to look at our situation, see where we can practice, where we can engage, and realize that aggression is the enemy of the dralas.

For example, I can be very attached to whether or not my tea is going to be exactly the right strength. When someone offers me tea, I might already have a low level of anger because it may not be exactly as I wish. That is setting sun, how we reduce our windhorse. Why is my mind like this? Why couldn't I look at my cup of tea and have equanimity? It doesn't really matter if the tea is cold or hot. Later, when I've drunk it, it isn't going to matter at all. My mind will have gone to the next thing.

As we live our lives, we can strengthen the life-force energy or we can weaken it. With lungta practice we are increasing it. Raising windhorse stimulates the body by bringing consciousness in; it brings focus into the heart and into the environment. Even though it's a profound practice, we can use it in a mundane way. If we're having difficulties, making important decisions, trying to overcome family obstacles and so forth, we can raise lungta with Ashe—the primordial stroke. *A* means "primordial," *she* means "to slice."

In Tibet, saying that someone has good lungta means they have a forward momentum to their demeanor. They are moving towards success. By success, we're not talking about being overly ambitious, but about accomplishing what we want. In the colloquial warrior language of Eastern Tibet, when things don't work out for someone we say that they have lost their windhorse, their ability to accomplish.

It all comes down to how we are able to hold Shambhala in our mind. These teachings show us how to cross over from understanding the transcendental quality of wisdom, to the actual practicality of engaging in life and making decisions at every level. The Great Eastern Sun is all-pervasive, forward thinking, and visionary. Connecting with its energy can bring inspiration and strength to our life.

With lungta, we become leaders; we become warriors; we become kings and queens—because we're able to bring about success and accomplishment. Then what we do begins to affect and inspire others. Our lungta becomes contagious. In the same way, engrained negativity begins to affect the environment. The core of the Shambhala teachings is that we must be able to live together in harmony. The key aspect of living together harmoniously is the discipline of each individual. When each individual has discipline and confidence, that begins to exude into the environment.

We use visualization and stroke practice to raise lungta, but the point is to take that energy out into the world. We want to go beyond ourselves. That going beyond is determined by how strong we feel. The warrior teachings emphasize steadiness, being consistent with our intention. Yet the environment of our particular dark age encourages fickleness. In fact, fickleness is almost a fashion. Fickle mind translates into doubt.

There are two kinds of doubt. The first is critical intelligence, which looks at something to see if it's true. Without that level of doubt, we're spineless, like jellyfish. But if pride takes over and we become obsessed with doubt, there's no joy. This second kind of doubt just feeds ego, the quality of maintaining "my thing." It is even possible to practice Ashe with the intent of perpetuating "my thing." As a matter of fact, in a dark age it is difficult not to do that.

As warriors we are being asked to liberate ourselves from that kind of shortsightedness. Ours is a path of sacredness that takes us beyond small mind. Bringing the primordial stroke of confidence into the heart center is a way to make us stronger. All beings from beginningless time have had the awakened quality. What is the essence of that? It is beyond concept and primordially good. Therefore we call it basic goodness, because it is the ground of all.

3

HOLDING THE VIEW

ELEMENTS OF ASHE

When we visualize the Ashe, we know that it stands for confidence in basic goodness, which is beyond manipulation. It is genuine mind. A genuine mind does not give in to our trips because it sees through our story line and habit. Sometimes it's hard for us to come up with that kind of confidence on the spot, so we have a format, a practice. We raise lungta by visualizing Ashe.

Lung is wind, *ta* is horse. Often when we want to do something we're overcome by fear and obstacles, which are usually coming from a mind that is reacting to the phenomenal world. Windhorse creates confidence in what lies beyond those appearances. It is more ultimate than worldly charisma. Windhorse brings wangthang, genuine presence—a field of power infused with ziji. That is how windhorse successfully expedites any wish.

So first we have *A*. In *The Torch of Certainty*, Mipham Rinpoche says that once we know *A*, we know all things. *A* is the primordial ground. Therefore it is the confidence of all. *A* has a quality of suchness, the ground nature, basic goodness. Because we have *A*, we see, we know. And what do we know? On a relative level, we know that sentient beings suffer. Sentient beings needlessly harm each other; we needlessly harm ourselves.

She is the stroke, the nature radiating out, giving birth to mercy and compassion. What is the ultimate *she* in the Ashe? The Dorje Dradül spoke of it as enlightened society. To bring about an enlightened world, a situation where compassion can be ultimately beneficial for the benefit of all sentient beings, is the path of Ashe.

In raising windhorse first we take the view of Ashe, and then we enact it in our body. We know what the Ashe represents, realize what is coming in, and allow it to cut through all the doubt: the klesha, the confusion, and the fear—a sense of losing our own compassionate activity. To quell the concepts that are coming up in our mind like arrows perpetually wounding us, we need something primordial, something that cannot be manipulated at all. The Ashe is like a diamond: it cannot be destroyed, but it can destroy. It is the glory—completely potent, completely prevalent, completely able to accomplish.

GOOD NEWS

The good news is that, fundamentally and unequivocally, there is basic goodness. Having confidence in basic goodness allows us to engage in life fearlessly. When we enact nonconceptual reality with our body by bringing the Ashe in, we are strengthening our confidence in the nature. It is not just the nature of me—"Oh, I'm basically good." *Everything* is basically good. That is the view of Shambhala.

At the beginning of Shambhala Training, when people hear about basic goodness, everybody asks, "What is that? Does it mean that everybody is good and then there is bad? I know some bad people, and they're not good." That view splits the concept of basic goodness into a contorted misunderstanding. Here we are talking about "good" in a completely unfabricated context. In Tibetan we say *döma-ne sangpo*. *Döma-ne* means beginningless. It is related to the word *ye-ne*, primordial. As the Dorje Dradül points out in his texts, this is the quality of the dawn of Vajrasattva, the completely embodied buddha who transmits the highest teachings.

The notion of beginningless is that you cannot find a fault in it. There is no time, because as soon as you have time involved it means that something is going to get worse or it is going to get better. In that case you could say, "Well, my basic goodness is pretty good right now, but it is going to get better."

The word *sangpo*, which is translated as "goodness," means "pure," "good," without any obscurations, defilements, or imperfections. That's referring to the fundamental quality of our mind and the environment. The teachings say that döma-ne sangpo is the primordial ground and that in the beginning beings don't trust it. From there we get the split between good and bad, which is ignorance—not understanding.

So when we say "good," we're not talking about good as opposed to bad or negative, but good as in primordial purity or cleanness. Even if we are obscured or a dichotomy is taking place, fundamentally the mind will always be that way—döma-ne sangpo. What we are presenting is a basic state of goodness from beginningless time.

Other teachings talk about *gewa* and *migewa*—virtue and nonvirtue—but this teaching transcends even that: if there is not really *basic* goodness, but goodness as opposed to badness, then it will come and go, and there will be perpetual warfare. In our practice we might have an experience of such goodness, but after practicing we might get confused about it and therefore do something negative. That doesn't mean we've lost our basic goodness. From that primordialness, the setting sun also comes out. That's why basic goodness is a very advanced teaching.

We're always struggling with this notion of goodness. It is almost as if we know that there is goodness, we can feel it, and we can sometimes experience it, but somehow we lose confidence in it. When we begin to lose confidence, we begin to plant solidity onto the situation. We begin to start fending for ourselves in a way that is probably not very helpful. As soon as we get up in the morning, if we don't trust that fundamental goodness, we act in a way to try to make up for it. That produces suffering and irritation. We start creating discrepancies between individuals, so we lose respect for some people and we encourage others. Then we have a war going on.

SEEING SACRED WORLD

In stroke practice, drinking the ink and planting the brush are ways of realizing confidence in the view of basic goodness. This brush is our sword, our sword of prajna. It is our weapon; we are touching it to the tongue. This ink is the Rigden's blood. When we execute the stroke we are receiving an empowerment, an *abhisheka*. We are receiving the ink on our tongue, and we drink it. In abhisheka we take a vow. If we break the vow, the oath water turns to molten iron. Here, in the same way, if we break our vow to use the mind of Ashe to experience basic goodness, we are going to choke on the ink.

It's not so much that the brush or the ink has power. We can't look at it in a mundane way. We are using these implements to empower us so that when we practice Ashe, we are developing confidence in the warrior's approach. We are developing confidence in enlightened society. We are developing confidence that we ourselves are the embodiment of basic goodness, right now and always.

As we obviously know, that confidence diminishes. The clouds come over and we begin to get depressed and sink into ourselves. Somehow we regard that depression or that sinking feeling as "real reality." We believe that once we get off cloud nine, that is really how things are. The great lineage of Shambhala practitioners tells us something entirely different. *The Letter of the Golden Key* talks about how the warriors of Shambhala enjoy themselves in the "ocean of butter and gold of great enriching-presence."

Gold is directly associated with *yün*, which the Dorje Dradül

called an "energy spot." It is also associated with Samanta-
bhadra—in Tibetan, Küntu Sangpo—the highest and most
perfect buddha within the *dzokchen* tradition. Küntu Sangpo's
golden field is perfect and pristine. There are theories about
where Küntu Sangpo lives, but in fact, when realized and accomplished, Küntu Sangpo is in our mind stream right now as
the gold-ness of the golden age of Shambhala.

THE GENUINE HEART OF SADNESS

We live in a society where each generation likes to improve
on how things were for the previous generation. But we can't
improve on the nature of reality. Basic goodness is why we are
here, and this is what we are practicing. We have to chew on it
continuously to see it for ourselves. Is it this way or is it that
way? Is it relative or is it absolute? Maybe it is the two together? Well, what's relative? And what is absolute? In my state of
mind right now, is this the true way of looking at it?

We have a genuine lineage. Lineage is not oppression. It is
not a matter of me telling you what the view is and your being
forced to believe it. We all have to deal with our understanding
and ask, "Is it really true?" We have to practice it ourselves until we can say, "Oh, it's true, there is something that is genuine
that has lasted through time that gets no better, neither does
it get any worse." That view is what we are inheriting in this
particular situation. It is a feeling of loyalty and faith, accom-
panied by great yearning. We are yearning to understand the
notion of complete awakening and complete awareness. When
we do, our world is not going to be good-er; it is just going to

be good and good, and it will always be that way.

In the Shambhala terma, this yearning is called "the genuine heart of sadness." Sadness here is a quality of loneliness, as opposed to depression. That feeling of being completely alone, the Dorje Dradül said, is lineage: our teacher and the lineage have experienced it. It is good to know that. Otherwise we will become overwhelmed and disheartened.

Sadness comes from having taken in all of reality. It is a soft, devotional sensibility, as if we are the parent of all sentient beings. Sadness is the sign of strength and openness. This yearning is the human element of calling to the dralas and to the mother and father lineages. It is the cord by which our enlightened quality is engaged.

ANTIDOTE FOR THE SETTING SUN

We like to talk about how the world is directing us toward awakening, but having our mind stopped in a moment of wakefulness doesn't do us any good unless we know what wakefulness is.

No matter what practice we are doing, we need to have the courage to look directly at our mind. The mind is the source of everything. If we are unable to relate to our mind, life becomes difficult, full of suffering and distraction. Warriorship is being unafraid to look at who we are. That doesn't mean trying to psychoanalyze our emotional state. Rather, we need to know how to unwind our own confusion. To bring our vision down to our immediate situation, we have to learn how to handle our mind, body, and speech.

First, it's important to relax and begin to step away from believing everything that comes into your mind. It's helpful just to watch your mind early in the morning and see how easy it is to follow every little thought. Before you go to sleep in the evening, replay your day, looking at where you got caught up. This practice results in a stronger sense of humor—you begin to see how silly it is, the way we hold on to thoughts.

In our speech, instead of regurgitating words that are useless, we can say words that are meaningful. The notion of chanting, for example, is to put profound words of wisdom in our minds and mouths. At the same time, if we're saying a chant and our mind is not there, the words will not have much power. It really comes down to our intention.

In our activities, we need to know deep within ourselves when we are on the path of warriorship and when we are taking an excursion to the side. Are we looping back? Are we sitting down on the trail, just hoping things get better?

Many of us fall into being possessed by doubt. Doubt can be a perpetual nuisance and ultimately undermine the warrior. One way to cut through that doubt is to remember the perspective of egolessness, of selflessness, which is Ashe. When we do that, the world of possibility begins to open up and we don't have to look for a tailor-made path.

We also need to support each other, engaging daily in developing our own windhorse, increasing our personal dralas, as well as gathering with friends and in groups to gather group energy and windhorse. As we gather our collective lungta, dignity, and doubtlessness about basic goodness, we will produce clouds of deathless *amrita*, the magical elixir that is the antidote for the setting sun. Shambhala has existed in one form or another for over 2500 years, and it has always come down to the principle of gathering for the welfare of others. Openhearted *bodhichitta* makes life joyous, harmonious, and delightful.

THE LEGACY OF DAWA SANGPO

The Dorje Dradül came to the West and emphasized the Shambhala teachings as a primary vehicle for us to establish a sane community. We are living in a very critical time, and much trust has been placed in our hands. The legacy of the past and hopefully the future is falling upon our heads. Thus we are forced to understand and practice these teachings at a quicker rate than we might have chosen. The alternative is to give into materialism and negativity. Already we see the magic of our world reduced to products that we are trying to buy and sell. This is not who we are. We are living breathing entities who must be connected to the physical earth and the literal sky. We have to look up sometimes.

It is said that Dawa Sangpo, the first king of Shambhala, after receiving the Kalachakra, or "Wheel of Time," initiation from the Buddha, recognized his own basic goodness on the spot, becoming a universal monarch, a completely enlightened ruler. He took the teachings to Shambhala and built a giant stupa. According to the Shambhala terma, he performed the stroke of Ashe. Then he began to propagate and teach the transmission he had received from the Buddha about basic goodness. Not only was it his personal practice, but it was also a view of social transformation, the understanding of which became the basis for all of Shambhala society. People slept, walked, ate, and worked according to the principle and understanding of their indestructible nature.

If people began to doubt this inherent goodness and confidence, they might leave the land of Shambhala—metaphorically or physically. They would roam into the kingdom of anger and pride, having lost the windhorse to see such kleshas as fickle, without any loyalty. Once pride and anger have departed, people look foolish, having believed their thoughts were real. Besides that, they have to clean up the karmic repercussions of activity rooted in such beliefs. Basic goodness is beyond karma. It does not fall into the pitfalls of being created or not being created. Thus basic goodness is the ideal foundation of an enlightened society.

The transformation that Dawa Sangpo effected for his kingdom began to influence all aspects of society, for it brought inspiration and meaning to people's lives. Without the principle of basic goodness, we engage in life with a narrow view. When the view is not rooted in a broader foundation of wisdom and mercy, we fall prey to aggression, jealousy, and desire, which lead us on. This lack of depth manifests as life without meaning or principle, life based on short-term goals for short-term satisfaction.

Without an understanding of the ground nature, basic goodness, people are more prone to the negativity of materialistic forces in the world. Even though these negative forces are ultimately within our own mind, they appear externally as well. With a shortsighted view, life becomes a continual battle in which we forsake our own dignity, which reduces our life force. Seeing these trends in his subjects, Dawa Sangpo encouraged them to increase drala by planting Ashe in the mind stream. Individual by individual, group by group, transformation began to take place.

Thus these principles, transmissions, and teachings became the guiding elements in Shambhala. Even in the name Dawa Sangpo, meaning "good moon," the principle of basic goodness is revealed. This process continued for a succession of seven dharma kings, at which point Jampal Trakpa, the first Rigden of Shambhala, empowered all Shambhala subjects with the Kalachakra, with the intention that they would all then be of one family—the family of vajra, of basic goodness. This is how Jampal Trakpa became the first Rigden king.

As citizens of Shambhala ourselves, not only do we become aware that basic goodness is the indestructible nature that underlies all life, but we wholeheartedly take possession of it. Rigden literally means "possessor of the family." What family? The family of basic goodness. In the family of basic goodness, we have Great Eastern Sun. The word "great" means that we are no longer mired in doubt, cowardice, and fear about our true nature. We have awakened to our basic goodness. "East" means that we can perpetually recognize it. This is what we are designed to do, and we can do it. "Sun" means that we il-luminate the path with this view.

The Buddha said that he can show us the path, but we are

the ones who must tread on it. "Path" sometimes connotes certainty in the view of basic goodness. Therefore the mahayana can be understood as great certainty and the vajrayana can be understood as indestructible certainty—or in Shambhala, Great Eastern certainty. All these paths lead to the same principle if we wholeheartedly engage in the view of basic goodness.

4
JOINING SPIRITUAL AND WORLDLY

JOINING SPIRITUAL AND WORLDLY

The Dorje Dradül often referred to the teachings of Shambhala
as being "secular." He meant that this teaching is a totality.
The secular and the spiritual are one: each depends on the
other. Not polarizing the sacred and the secular is known as
"all-victorious."

The Shambhala teachings are very daring. When we use the
word "sacred," we are not talking about leaving or transcend-
ing the world. At this time, we don't have the luxury to be
yogis in caves. Our practice is to discover the magic within the
realm of worldly existence. That is the notion of totality. We
are fully involved, a hundred percent, using all aspects of life
as implements for awakening.

The totality of Shambhala involves an element of giving in.
Our habit is to build a barricade and obtain what we can from
the conventional. These teachings are saying that victory and

power—both spiritual and worldly—come from egolessness. They come from the absence of privacy—not scurrying away to hide in a corner of our mind. Our whole life is the path; all of it is offered.

In this way, the secular nature of the Shambhala teachings goes against convention: we usually think we'll lose freedom if we give up comfort or privacy. But I have studied with some very great teachers—in my experience the most surrendered people—and I notice that they seem to be more free and intelligent than the rest of us.

Even when we're meditating, it is possible to find ourselves not wanting to surrender to the clear light; we'd rather be sitting in our thoughts with what is comfortable or entertaining. This is how a coward behaves, falling back into the habit of seeking pleasure. Destructive patterns can invade our life without our knowing it. In part of Gesar's story he gets seduced and falls into a stupor. After three years he wakes up and says, "What am I doing? I am just lying around perpetuating the same habitual patterns." And that's Gesar.

When we hear about the mythical Shambhala kingdom, we hear that its inhabitants have higher faculties, finely tuned sense perceptions. That's because those beings are no longer stuck at the level of chasing their insatiable desire for pleasure. Their state of mind is finer, more open to reality. It takes courage to access that kind of consciousness.

Victory over war involves having confidence to proclaim the truth, with no hesitation. When we hesitate, it is as if there are still pockets of fear in our life and we are trying to hide in those pockets. Those pockets need to be excavated. From a Shambhala warrior's point of view, that means having the fearlessness to face up to how things are. Such courage will break us free from the laziness in our mind. Then we will begin to see what the Shambhala terma is saying: we already have all the enlightened qualities, totally. Windhorse is very much the notion of trusting the situation.

The practicality of these teachings is real. As we begin to trust more in the Ashe in our heart, we're not as dependent on external situations. We're no longer trying to grasp mirages. Therefore we begin to be free from deception. We are no longer being deceived because we are no longer trying to hide from ourselves. There's the notion of giving in.

TAKING A LEAP

Windhorse is a quality of riding the consciousness—the mind, the *sem*, the *rig* in Rigden—the sacredness that is displayed everywhere. The mind is sacred, we are sacred, and the world is sacred. The point of raising lungta is to wake up and see the sacredness. We are all going through life with windhorse as a possibility.

When *The Letter of the Black Ashe* says, "Warriors and cowards," it is talking about the moment when we decide how we are going to regard the world—as dead or alive, available or not, conditioned or unconditioned. When we say, "I wish this would change, I wish that would change," we are misbelieving our perceptions. We think that changing our mirages is going to lead somewhere. Because in our particular time it is difficult to trust basic goodness, our whole life may consist of continuously searching for happiness in one unsatisfied thought after another. We ordinarily use these thoughts to fortify our self, hoping that something good will happen.

With prajna—that razor-sharp quality of knowing—we can cut through our ignorance to a level of lungta and confidence. These are omnipresent, always available, always happening. The technique is to access them directly and simply by visualizing the Ashe. This is how we cut through obstacles and engage in any activity with lungta, the mind that is not depressed.

With the practice of Ashe, we are taking a leap. We are cutting through any kind of hesitation that comes about by completely trusting our prajna and windhorse. With that we have an extension of great compassion. That is how we are going to build Shambhala—not with mind tricks or by making things complicated, but by utilizing what is available. That is what the Dorje Dradül means by being fully involved.

RELATIVE AND ABSOLUTE

From an early age the Dorje Dradül took great pride in a certain aspect of teaching. He said, "I am in the lineage where I do not separate relative and absolute. They are completely unified." On the one hand that's a very simple statement. But if we think about it in terms of our practice, especially here in the West, we are often in a hurry to experience the absolute. It may be that we're in pain or we're having a hard time relating with what's going on, so we want to see what's ultimately behind it. But if we get too far from the relative, it's going to be hard to understand the ultimate.

The Tibetan word for "relative" means that everything is covered. What is covered? The absolute is covered. And what is covering it? Our ignorance, our misunderstanding. The most dramatic of these misunderstandings is the concept of the self. We take this body, speech, and mind, wrap it all together, and say it's a self, a thing, an existence. With this root misunderstanding, we perpetuate worldly ways.

On a relative level, it appears that things exist. Ultimately, they don't exist in the way we think. But we can't simply say that ultimately they don't exist and relatively it doesn't matter. It does matter, in a relative sense. There is a relative "me," a relative self—a person with an address and a phone number—so it's important to take care of ourselves and to behave virtuously.

As warriors engaging in the relative world, we are deepening our mind with the absolute, our view of basic goodness. That is how we develop the space of equanimity. We can begin to test our understanding of the ultimate by seeing how we react to the relative. For example, when we encounter praise or blame, if we understand the deeper meaning we understand that praise is relative, and therefore so is blame. There is really no one to praise, no one to blame. If our mind spins off and gets happy when we're praised and upset when we're blamed, we're still living in a superficial way. Seeing only the relative, we take it as the absolute, as opposed to seeing the absolute nature of the relative.

What is fortunate about our situation is that within the relative, there is the ultimate, wisdom, shining through the dark like a beacon of light. When we use relative appearances to embody compassion and kindness, concern for others, and virtue, that beacon of light becomes stable and strong.

THE BIG PICTURE

Even if we're thinking in a very short-term way, we need to remember the nature of the big picture: The ground nature is basic goodness and every situation is basic goodness. No matter what is taking place, the ground nature is always the same. Otherwise the teachings are not true or consistent, neither are they diamond-like.

We think that on the day we realize our intrinsic nature we'll know more, but we won't know any more. Nothing will have changed. If enlightenment involved increase or decrease, time or place, awakening to our own wisdom would be an extreme state of spirituality, a self-concocted religion. We would have divided samsara and nirvana. In the terma, the Dorje Dradül talks about nirvana and samsara as hope and fear.

The reason the Ashe vibrates is that it creates samsara and nirvana simultaneously. That's what we call co-emergent. The warrior is courageous because the warrior does not give into misconception that would see it otherwise. Doubt-free mind is another way of looking at it.

A doubt-free mind is devotion, which the Dorje Dradül often equated with loyalty, or steadiness. Such a mind can access basic goodness and rest there more easily and quickly. That doubtlessness has a correlation to our everyday life. If we have doubt about the basic goodness of our own friends and family, then it's very difficult to have doubtlessness in our meditation experience. So in the Shambhala sense, doubtlessness also means having a level of decency and respect for others.

Shambhala is a wisdom culture. Our view is balanced in the sense of knowing that the world is not dead and recognizing its energies as part of being alive. That's what a wisdom culture is—one that understands the notion of spirit. As Shambhala warriors in this modern world, we understand that the notion of spirit has been lost and we are reintroducing it. Therefore we no longer lose ourselves in everyday actions, becoming mindless with speed or forgetfulness. We do not get into the game of hope and fear because we no longer get hooked on worldly dharmas. That is how we join heaven and earth.

Raising windhorse, we are crossing into the path of wisdom, which is always available to us. We are carrying the profound into the mundane. We have looked at how things are and seen that yes, the ground of being is basic goodness. Appearances are endowed with a quality of suchness. In our mind right now, basic goodness has not increased or decreased one iota. We can relax on the spot, knowing the nature to be primordial and complete. On the path of wisdom, we are unimpeded, able to engage with the world in an honest way.

II
TRUST IN THE SACRED WORLD

5

GETTING FROM HERE
TO HERE

THE ASHE PRACTICE and the whole path, for that matter, are based upon our understanding of basic goodness. Do we or do we not understand basic goodness? Do we or do we not understand that the nature of mind and the nature of all situations is primordial, beginningless, stainless, and without any bounds?

When the Dorje Dradül received the terma of the Ashe, the Rigdens said, "Here is a practice that will help you further understand the principle of the ground nature." Just as every ray of the sun hits a different spot and looks different from every angle, just so there are many methods by which we can experience basic goodness and the kingdom of Shambhala. These methods are our weaponry of compassion.

BEGINNING WITH THE RELATIVE

The Shambhala teachings refer to both relative and absolute

Ashe. The black Ashe is relative Ashe. Visualizing it is a method by which we gain confidence, certainty, and unequivocal determination that basic goodness is the basis of all. Frankly, right now most of us don't believe this, even if we mouth the words. The reason we do not have inspiration to meditate and work with our mind is that, fundamentally, we think it is unworkable. We think that, fundamentally, we are stuck: "No matter how much butter I put on the toast, it's burnt. It's always going to be burnt and there is nothing I can do about it." That's our attitude: we're trying to doctor up something that we think is not workable. Even though we may have a feeling for basic goodness and we say that all the reasons make sense, innately we're not sure that we really trust the situation.

The Letter of the Black Ashe says that there were warriors and there were cowards. The cowards ran away, not trusting the ground nature. To be warriors, we need to trust our basic goodness. The tool we have for doing that is Ashe. We know that *A* means primordial, unfabricated, completely undoctored. It is beyond any kind of description. The actualization of basic goodness is a nonconceptual state beyond interpretation. All you can frankly say about it is *A*. *She*, which means stroke, is the ability of that profound nature to strike and penetrate anywhere. This is its embodiment, its all-victorious quality. It conquers all.

The principle of Ashe is so high, so subtle, so profound, that none of us can relate to it immediately, even though it is everywhere. That's why even though the relative and absolute Ashe are inseparable, we begin with the relative. When we practice black Ashe, we are using a relative manifestation of the ground nature as a meditative journey. It may sound as if we are talking about another planet, but we are talking about the nature of our own mind, the nature of all phenomena. When someone asks, "Who are you?" we might answer, "Well, I like the color blue and 'Gladiator' is my favorite movie." When we're raising windhorse by visualizing Ashe, we're saying, "I am Ashe. Ashe is the nature of who I am."

In a visualization practice like Ashe, we learn that the appearances produced by the mind can be of benefit if the appearance has meaning. When we do this practice, we need a clear understanding of the visualization as well as some understanding of the nature of mind. The nature of our mind may be displayed in many ways, but Ashe is the fundamental basis. We access basic goodness through the Ashe.

It is important that we don't get stuck on just the visual image of Ashe, but infuse it with the meaning that it represents. In a meditation practice like this we are bringing meaning and image together. This has to do with the notion of relative karma. We are all living in a relative situation, and anything that happens to us is either physical or mental karma. With Ashe we're in the course of changing that karma, using the most profound mechanism that has been given to us: visualization practice. Visualization practice is higher than just basic shamatha practice, because what we are visualizing is closer to reality, an expression of confidence in our fully awakened manifestation. When we visualize the Ashe, we know that it stands for confidence in reality beyond manipulation, and we embody those qualities.

When we dissolve the Ashe to overcome any fixation on the form, we experience the transcendental wisdom aspect by resting in basic goodness. That is how we manifest as absolute, ultimate Ashe. Relative and ultimate are happening all the time and simultaneously.

In *The Golden Sun of the Great East*, A is described in many ways. All the words describe the situation so that we realize that there is nothing beyond A. There is nothing that it could or could not do. It's beyond all that. The *she* is the potency. A has *she*, the ability to strike, to be compassionate, to be wrathful. Ashe has the ability to do anything. That is the notion of ultimate.

We might want the ultimate Ashe to be more relative. We'd like to be able to play around with it a little bit, make it a little more cute. The *she* would get very upset about that. It would cut that desire to get cozy. It is the protector of the truth, the drala of the truth. When our mind tries to grapple with ultimate Rigden principle and it can't hold on, that is absolute Ashe performing its duty completely. Our responsibility is to relax into the A, saying, "This is not a foe. This is drala trying to uplift me, raising me up."

PLANTING ASHE

Raising windhorse is the practice of visualizing the Ashe in front of us and saying, "I am bringing the mind of the Rigdens into my own mind and planting it in my heart." In doing this, we're saying that we have awakened to our true heart and mind. When this black Ashe descends into our heart center, it is the basis by which we are going to tread on the path of Shambhala.

Planting the Ashe is similar to the notion of *tathagatagarbha*—buddha nature or awakened nature—or *sugatagarbha*, which means "having gone to bliss." Buddha nature does not strictly refer to the historical Buddha, but to the awakened nature of all. The whole point of the journey is for us to take our seemingly ordinary body and make it buddha, awake. How do we do that?

In some traditions one has to purify and receive the awakened nature from an outside source. Our tradition is saying that the basis of our being is innate and we are seeing it as the Rigden king. This is the opportunity for us to manifest fully in the family of Rigden, possessor of the awareness of the highest family. Our genuine family is the completely liberated, unbiased Ashe. What does that mean? It means, "I myself am the Rigden. I am awake. That is my nature and that is what Ashe is saying. Now it's planted." It all comes down to this point.

We all sit and do our practices thinking, "How can I get from here to there?" That's the wrong way to think about it. The question is, "How can we get from here to here?" We're already here. This is where it is. There is no "there." If we think we need to get from here to there, it's never going to happen, because every time we go "there," we are getting further away from "here." This is a very important point in understanding how practice works.

We don't understand this little step because we are always

walking away from "here." That is why we visualize the Ashe coming toward us and then plant it in our heart. Sometimes it is referred to as a child being born. How is a child born? Mother and father come together. How is this child born? Basic goodness and the Great Eastern Sun, the ultimate Ashe, are joined to produce this child—relative Ashe. In this practice, we are bringing these elements into union. Thus the whole world is in union. The temporal world is the continual outplay of this union taking place. It is not a physical situation, but a consciousness that has to be understood.

Joy is the result of understanding this union, because we realize that the elements have never been separated. All of us naturally want joy—not temporary joy, not conditioned joy, but meek, perky, outrageous, inscrutable joy. Even on our deathbed we say, "I want joy." Eating a simple sandwich, we say, "I want joy." That's basic goodness speaking.

TRANSMITTING AWAKENMENT

When the Ashe descends into our being, we are enacting something that has already taken place. We're visualizing this because we have to generate a picture of how things really are, which we don't quite believe. We are doing it to convince ourselves. We might ask, "Couldn't I just visualize a cup coming into my head?" Perhaps if we have really good intentions, that might work. But a warrior who has actually accomplished something has given us this method. He says that it works. That's what we mean by preciousness. Even in a conventional sense, when we're looking to somebody else for a helpful tip, we're likely to take an experienced person's advice over a beginner's.

People often say that we all have buddha nature. Buddha nature is particularly a mahayana term, but it is used throughout the tantras. *Dewar shek-pe nyingpo* or sugatagarbha means "the heart or essence of going into bliss or joy." *Dewa* means bliss. *Nyingpo* is essence. There are many different words for the same thing. Even in the Buddhist context, sometimes this term is not understood clearly. The phrase refers to something that is within our body and consciousness right now. "Having gone to bliss" is a description of the cause of a result. It's like telling a small child, "One day you will be president," or "You can be a champ," when we see the child's potential. Here it is having gone to bliss. That is what buddha nature means. We have gone to bliss and that bliss has been planted in our being.

Perhaps we think, "Am I not fully buddha, or I am a little buddha and going to get to be a bigger buddha? Am I a little Rigden king and going to get to be a bigger Rigden king? What's going on?" We're saying that our understanding of Rigden is little, but our accomplishment is great. We're saying that once we plant that Ashe, we will definitely become an enlightened being. Our ability to do that is dependent on knowing that the awakened nature is already in us. Awakening to basic goodness is a transmission of what we already are. That is why this particular transmission has been handed down through our lineage.

Sometimes the Dorje Dradül referred to the black Ashe as embryonic. We have been born. We saw that moment when the Ashe was planted in our heart, and now we are just like a child who wants to grow up. Here we are, and we're going to get bigger and bigger. As our understanding of the ground nature grows, our confidence expands.

Suppose someone tells us there's a lotus in the pond. We don't see any lotuses anywhere, until one day we get the lotus empowerment by watching as someone plants a lotus in the pond. What's going to happen after that? Every day we are going to look and remember that we saw the lotus planted. We know it is there. When it rains, we know the lotus is growing and growing. We come to the same point when we have actualized Ashe.

6
OBSTACLES TO WINDHORSE

WHEN WE RISE IN THE MORNING and go about our day, it is important that we are able to see the world through the eyes of a warrior and express ourselves as a warrior. That is confidence.

Warriorship is a process of reflection, seeing how true these teachings are, testing our basic goodness over and over again. A key aspect of warriorship is having sadness and faith. Sadness is devotion to the Shambhala principles. Faith is understanding what we are doing and why we are doing it. Without sadness and faith we are perpetually dragged down to the lower realms of existence: our mind is reduced to fraternizing with aggression and passion, delusion and attachment.

What drags us down? *Pakchak*—habitual patterns. For lifetimes, an eternity, we have habitually been cowards—subhuman in a sense—because we have not risen to our potential. Lifetime after lifetime we have not risen to the possibility of being a true Shambhala warrior. Rising to our potential would be enlightened pakchak.

The golden age of Shambhala is right now. The essence of the whole Shambhala tradition is developing the confidence to trust in the sacred world. What is a sacred world? It is seeing basic goodness. Instead of saying, "This is real," and "That is not real," it is having the courage to see the purity and equality of the entire situation.

Having confidence in our true nature as basic goodness elevates us to being warriors of Shambhala. Yet sometimes we hesitate to act that way. If we do not understand the direction or purpose of the journey—if we do not have a map, so to speak—we spend a lot of time spinning in circles, not practicing properly in the right direction. What is it that we need to overcome? What are the impediments to windhorse?

AMBITION

First of all, we must overcome ambition—trying to accomplish something. When our mind is trying to accomplish something, it's because there is a sense of dissatisfaction, a lack of contentment. Ambition is different from exertion and practicing correctly. We could see it as the gears and wheels that keep samsara going. In wanting to make something happen, we are not recognizing basic goodness. We are not understanding who we are. Since we don't trust our nature, we perpetuate the continual, endless cycle. The Tibetan word for samsara is *khorwa*, "circular." We keep going around in a circle without having accomplished anything. We feel that we

are getting somewhere, but later we see that we have gotten
nowhere. There is always a sense of gain and loss.

Ambition is a sign that we are trying to appease our suffering by thinking that something external will make us happy.
Fundamentally that approach is ego-centered and aggressive.
It will never appease the suffering; it will always just fire it up.
Ambition that looks for some other situation has no intelligence. This kind of ambition is actually bewilderment. In Tibetan we say *timuk*. Timuk is not knowing what to do or where
to put our faith.

In contrast, the practice of Ashe is marked by genuine sadness and faith, which come from devotion and compassion.
We are devoted not only to the teacher but also to helping
others. We know that this activity is worthy of refuge. As we
open up our mind, we increase our ability to overcome aggression, and we have more and more devotion. This gives us faith
that when we put our ambition in this enlightened context, it
will actually materialize as something of value.

Conventionally speaking, every day we are putting our hope
and ambition into all kinds of things, coming up empty-hand-
ed. Meditation and postmeditation heighten our awareness
of the qualities of a worthy object. That is why we do formal
meditation practice. As warriors in this particular kingdom,
sitting meditation is our ground. It is having the courage to
literally take our seat and work with our mind. It is an essential method for cultivating lack of ambition in a positive sense:
we can relax into who we are.

ATTACHMENT

Another obstacle to realization, as taught by great teachers like Milarepa and Patrul Rinpoche, is attachment to one's family and friends. We have to let go of that sense of closeness, of fixation, of being caught in some kind of karmic situation with others. That attachment only creates suffering for ourselves and those around us. As a result we lose our ability to raise lungta. So in our mind we have to let go of those worldly concerns. As Shambhala practitioners, we can relate to our family and friends without holding on.

Or course we want our family and friends to be happy, but when we're caught up in our desire for things to go well, there's often a kind of aggression or greed at work. This is the mind of cowardice that *The Letter of the Black Ashe* is referring to. When it talks about the multitudes of cowards hiding themselves in caves and jungles, that's a metaphor for what takes place when attachment, aggression, or other heavy negative emotions take over. We forget about basic goodness and think we have to use klesha to get what we want. Then we begin to indulge in activities that jeopardize our windhorse.

In a dharmic culture we recognize that if we want our loved ones to be well, to practice well is the most beneficial thing we can do. In Tibetan culture when people are having family problems, getting married, or starting a new business, they supplicate a lama to perform some practices on their behalf. We might think that's spiritual materialism, but what do we usually do at such a time? We get mad at somebody; we seduce somebody; we try to manipulate the situation in order to get what we want. That approach doesn't work. In fact, it gets us even more entangled in attachment.

When the Dorje Dradül suggested to people who were having family or livelihood difficulties that they practice hard or go on a retreat, he wasn't just trying to keep us out of trouble. He was saying that if we practice hard, something in there is going to help. If we're going to be attached, it's better to be attached to practice. In practicing Ashe we are switching allegiance from the setting sun to the Great Eastern Sun. But we can't just get on the windhorse with gusto and hope for the best. We need to understand the power and dynamic of the practice. When we switch our allegiance and begin to trust the innate potency of our mind and heart, then automatically we are riding the horse. As we continue to rely on the practice, we're being reminded of what we already know, step by step.

If we're truly courageous and brilliant, we don't need any of these practices; we can raise lungta spontaneously. But most of us need a little guidance and direction. So out of compassion, those who have gone before us have given us some hints. When we manifest with brilliance, genuineness, confidence, and compassion, what do we call that? The Dorje Dradül is saying, "There's a primordial quality to it, and that's the Ashe." When we're going through life in this way, how does it feel? It feels like being on the back of a horse. We have expediency and forward momentum.

These hints are all helpful for us. Otherwise we start slipping into the opposite manifestation. We visualize having no wisdom, no creativity. We visualize all our problems in front, coming in, flipping around, and entering our heart, where we hold on to them tightly. The result of that visualization is stress, worry, and doubt. Then we extend that out to other individuals.

On the one hand, the Ashe visualization is very simple; on the other, it has a profound effect on our life. Mindfulness, the principle of the tiger, teaches us to be careful in a good way because we are powerful individuals and therefore we have to be aware of how we are manifesting and how we are relating to our mind and heart. If we shift our attention in just a few key ways, it's easy to fall into negativity. If we shift our attention in other key ways, it's easy to go in a positive direction.

FEAR, DEPRESSION, AND LAZINESS

Another obstacle to overcome is fear. When we are doing stroke practice and raising windhorse, we often think that we have to overcome something. For example, when we're going to a job interview, we think, "I need to raise windhorse." In doing that, are we trying to conquer the person interviewing us? Are we trying to put out a good feeling for them? No, we are trying to conquer our own doubt and fear. That fear stems from a lack of trust in our genuine being, which comes from ignorance of who we are. If we come from ignorance, we start thinking that we are real, that we have to perform, and that there are things to gain and lose. We have ambition.

Another obstacle is depression. Somehow we cannot get our energy up. Depression has the quality of doubt, of not really being able to engage or believe basic goodness to be true. It also has the quality of claustrophobia—we are comfortable only within our own limited domain of who we think we are and what we think we understand. We don't want to extend ourselves. Depression is related to laziness, and these two make a nice couple at the party of suffering. There's a low-grade anger involved, a slight irritation that others are celebrating. We want what they have. We need to liberate that sense of heaviness and depression.

It is said that both depression and wisdom can enter through our eye. If we begin to relax into the eye of wisdom, we are unimpeded in sacred view. But if we gaze out in a fixated, serious way, the world begins to look stuffy and congested. Depression sets in. That depression hinders windhorse; our lungta can be degraded and lost. We're not necessarily talking about clinical depression, but about the depression of our ability to perceive the world as it is. We have padded our perceptions. When we do this, how we engage in the world entraps us further in disbelief of our own Ashe. It is almost as if radar goes out and bounces back. We feel the room as small and the world as dead. So we have to relax in terms of how we regard our environment—obviously not in a sloppy way. Appreciating where we are right now is a helpful antidote to depression. Appreciation is another virtue of the tiger.

When we have overcome ambition, depression, and fear, we might still mistrust our basic goodness. There is subtle residual ambition, trying to get what we can out of this world while we're here. We are so accustomed to being consumed by fear, and so driven by the need to feed that fear, that we might have an impulse to continue in that way. Coming back to the practice of raising Ashe quells our fear and diminishes our self-involvement. We create a powerhouse, and we can extend ourselves from there.

7
Subjugating the Enemies

CUTTING THROUGH WITH ASHE

With the practice of Ashe, we have the opportunity to cut hesitation and fear at its root in order to see what is genuine. To do this we have to trust the Ashe that has been planted. As we invoke the Ashe, we are invoking the embodiment of basic goodness, nonconceptuality, and dignity. When we visualize it, we practice seeing something that is exterior coming through our forehead and going to our heart center. As it goes down, it is destroying ego; it is killing the sense of falsity or delusion.

The violence of the Ashe coming down is obviously a non-aggressive violence. We are cutting and destroying for the benefit of all sentient beings and for the benefit of this and future kingdoms. We are saying, "For the future, I need to squash this doubt that I have genuine lungta. Otherwise I will find myself subject to another kingdom very shortly." Is there something physical that we are killing? No. We are destroying doubt; we are killing confusion.

Doubt and confusion are ways of suffering in the lower realms. As long as we are living in those other kingdoms, we are doing a sort of negative lungta practice all the time. For example, we see something in a store and we visualize it coming towards us. We think, "Oh, I am going to feel much better when I have that; everyone will think I am great, and I will think I am great." We see that article of clothing and visualize it coming into us, and we pay the money. This regular kind of materialistic lungta is very short-lived. That's what we are killing and destroying.

The practice we are doing in Shambhala is beyond just this world. Shambhala world is continuous. One of the qualities of the Rigden is genuine permanence. It goes from moment to moment, lifetime to lifetime, forever.

LIBERATING FEARLESSNESS

The Letter of the Black Ashe talks about how out of the cosmic mirror—out of space, we could say—were created multitudes of beings. Some of those beings became warriors, like the Rigden kings and Shiwa Ökar. Multitudes of others embodied as confused beings who did not trust their own lungta. Those beings manifested in the way of beginning and end—eternalism and nihilism. When we raise windhorse, Ashe descends as the condensed energy, realization, and understanding of the Rigden king—beginningless and endless, quaking with presence. With Ashe we are killing the basis of confusion, the concept of beginning and end.

In stroke practice, we first invoke the lineage so that the continuity of courage and blessings comes through. We are practicing putting thought and intention into the brush, which is like a sword in the way we execute the stroke. As we bring down the brush, we might have certain hesitations or feelings about what is going on. It may not necessarily be about a person or situation we're having trouble with, but there's a general energy. As we do that, we're saying, "How do I deal with that situation? I deal with it by invoking these dralas and virtues." As we continue making the stroke, we see the obstacles being overcome and removed by the tiger, lion, garuda, and dragon principles. We're also engaging our ability to be genuine, true, and vast—all these elements. We're holding the brush and infusing our mind with the ability to do these things.

We call it the black Ashe because it's relative; it's a tangible thing. Black has many meanings; one of them is engaging in the ability to overcome. We don't have to visualize that we're stabbing somebody's head; that would be a little excessive. It would only result in our getting more upset. Rather, we're invoking the lineage, seeing the obstacles, overcoming them, and emerging with an all-victorious quality.

People have asked why the Shambhala deities such as the Rigdens are dressed as warriors and kings and queens and so on. That element indicates activity and being in the world. In Tibetan it's called *thin-le*, or buddha activity, enlightened activity. Why are some deities peaceful? Why are some very wrathful? Just as in life, we need different ways of dealing with things.

With Ashe we are using an activity with a very strong benevolent energy to overcome all obstacles. That's not easy to do, so we're going through the process of cultivating the ability in our own private realm. It can be helpful to ask, "What is my intention? I want to overcome this obstacle, but by using what means?" We want to be using the elements of wisdom and compassion. When we rouse the black Ashe, we are physically overcoming hesitation and liberating those elements of fearlessness.

III
THE DRALAS ARE HERE

8
BEING GENUINE

WHAT ABOUT BASIC GOODNESS?

For most of our lives we have been slaves to the influences of aggression, perpetual discursiveness, and desire; we have not been free from those tethers. Our mind is handed off like a baton from aggression to passion to ignorance and then when they are done, jealousy comes along and says, "Now I'll take over for a while." As warriors, we see that this situation is not genuine. We see that underneath it all is basic goodness. *That* is genuine.

This is a profound understanding. We are dividing it up—into relative and absolute Ashe, into the principles of court, into the higher, intermediate, and mundane dralas, into the four dignities—so that we are able to perceive it. This is all a way of tuning in to the energy of basic goodness—how things are when we trust our own nature. We are describing the journey of trusting the awakened mind that we already possess. As we begin to trust, we realize that our path is already laid out in front of us, manifesting wherever we go. We can see this at the relative level of using cups and saucers, wearing clothing and uniforms, and working with the inner aspects of how we hold our mind. At the root of it all is basic goodness.

I am trying to perpetually hit people over the head with the notion of basic goodness. My hope is that if we actually hear the word, we might wake up in the middle of the night and contemplate it. Instead of contemplating what happened at work, we might say, "Hmm, what about basic goodness?" That is how we train as warriors, by changing the percentage of set-ting-sun thoughts versus Great Eastern Sun thoughts in our mind stream. Considering that every day we have thousands of thoughts, it really is a choice. How many of our thoughts are bringing us down to a lower situation, and how many are lifting us up?

RECOGNIZING THE GENUINE

The Shambhala teachings have a sense of immediacy, which they share with the vajrayana path. In conventional Buddhist logic we have quite a reasonable amount of time to get en-lightened—billions of lifetimes. We can practice at a nice pace and put ourselves on cruise control for a while—eventually we will get there. On the vajrayana path we can become enlight-ened in one lifetime. Shambhala is just as immediate. We have to accomplish it now. We talk about dralas as war gods and how, especially at this time, we have to do something.

To do this, we need to recognize the importance of confidence and windhorse within our mind stream. That is why I am emphasizing drala. *Dra* means "enemy," and *la* means "to transcend," "to be above." Drala is unequivocal; it does not give in. We can look at a situation and try to talk ourselves into it—"Oh, that looks like an uplifted situation." Drala says, "No, that is laziness, fear, hesitation. You can do better than that." Drala protects what is genuine and innate.

The Shambhala warrior is on a continual field trip of considering what is genuine. Every thought that comes up, we can ask, "Is this genuine or not?" We can do the same with our behavior, our activity. Discerning what is genuine is very much a process of looking at what to cultivate and what to discard, which is the first stage of how to raise proper windhorse, how to have confidence. It is not a matter of having confidence and just jumping in. We have to be very discerning in terms of our ability and our situation. Therefore we cultivate the four dignities.

A PERSONAL JOURNEY

Genuineness comes from increasing our understanding. There will be times when we're less confident and we'll make mistakes—but that's not really our concern. Our concern is how we can go forward. For most of us, when push comes to shove in our life, the first thing we drop is the dharma. We go back to our habitual way. But that's precisely the time we should be trying to apply the principles of warriorship.

As we study more and move along, we might have doubts about those principles; it is important to understand the doubt and process it. Then we can use those principles as the main vehicle by which we engage. This is part of the excitement of being on the journey: we're testing ourselves, observing how these principles work. We need to think long-term.

Deep down we know that there is some enlightened wisdom that we all have; otherwise we wouldn't be here. Every great teacher, every sage and buddha who has gone beyond, has told us this. In the process of discovering it, we go through a lot of doubt. This is a personal journey: we shouldn't base it on expecting certain results. We can only see for ourselves what will happen if we follow the instructions. We are often very goal-oriented, fruition-oriented. Warriorship is less about fruition and more about path. Being on the journey is a process of becoming confident in our genuineness.

CONFIDENCE IN WHAT IS REAL

In order to make our understanding more genuine, less doubt-ridden, and more sophisticated, we sharpen the Ashe. Of course the Ashe doesn't really get sharper, but in the process of our practice, it *seems* like it's getting sharper. We start with really basic activities—how to dress, how to have a conversation, how to have a decent shrine. As we continue to practice, we are building confidence. I truly feel that this is why the Dorje Dradül presented these particular teachings, not only as an expression of his own journey, but as a gift and transmission to us all. He was showing us that the difference between ourselves and the ultimate warrior—the ultimate Rigden, the Sakyong, the Buddha, whatever language you want to use—is having confidence in what is real.

As warriors we begin to reflect on our own mind and heart; we taste the ink as we perform the Ashe. We touch the brush to our tongue and the ink penetrates our whole being. This is pure Rigden wisdom. We are taking in that Rigden wisdom and planting it in our heart center. Then the glorious and rich mind of the golden age dawns. "Golden" represents the sense of complete liberation and freedom. It is the perpetual arising of the Great Eastern Sun.

Once we have tasted the Rigdens' blood, once we have experienced even a little bit of nonconceptuality, we can fly like the garuda, who is so happy flying that it doesn't even look for a place to land. In that space, the garuda meets the dragon. Down below, it sees the snow lion and the tiger.

We can look at the path in terms of these creatures, who represent methods of confidence by which we become warriors. The dralas of meek, perky, outrageous, and inscrutable protect the space of egolesslessness and spontaneity. These four kinds of confidence are the vanguards and the vehicle of enlightenment. These dignities represent our activity as warriors. The fruition of this process is being able to leap into a realm beyond fixation.

9

THE DIGNITY OF MEEK

THE FIRST STAGE of rousing confidence is the tiger, the dignity of meek. Meekness is related to gewa, virtue, and *sönam*, merit. We are talking about what to cultivate and what to discard. Cultivating virtue and accumulating merit is how we gather fuel for windhorse.

Obviously, the buddhadharma also emphasizes cultivating virtue. These traditions cross over at many points. In the mahayana teachings we rouse bodhichitta and take a vow to work for the benefit of all sentient beings for limitless lifetimes to appease their needs and quell their suffering. We heard about tathagatagarba and sugatagarba—planting buddha nature in the heart and having gone to bliss. The Shambhala tradition has very much to do with this aspect of energy.

We could even say that mahayana Buddhism is borrowing from the tradition of Shambhala warriorship; it is the melding of these two traditions. Shantideva makes a correlation between bodhichitta and warriorship. Bodhichitta is the part of sem, mind, that is willing to be courageous. In Shambhala, there is a correlation between our willingness to be courageous and our desire to engage with the world.

VIRTUE AND FRIENDLINESS

As we proceed on the path of the warrior, meek is how we are able to discern what drala is. We are often confused about that. Looking at the world through the eyes of aggression and desire obscures the openness of our mind. The way we remove the obscurations is by developing virtue.

Ultimately, we talk about the notion of basic goodness, which is beyond good and bad. To understand the goodness, we have to develop a deeper wisdom. The way to access that is by virtue. So we make a vast gathering of the dralas of virtue. To do this, we take the path of meekness, tiger, which emphasizes mindfulness.

To be meek is to know what the world has to offer. It is to understand that as warriors—practitioners and budding Rigdens—we have to be very sensitive to our environment. We need to know what we can take on and what we cannot take on. As *The Letter of the Black Ashe* says, "The warriors who are meek/Are friendly to themselves and merciful to others."

"Friendly to ourselves" is a good motto. It starts with discerning what to cultivate and what to discard. Should we have animosity towards ourselves? Should we let ourselves indulge in laziness? It is very much a meditative journey.

One way we are friendly ourselves is to practice *shamatha*, the ability to sit down and relax in peace, to take a break from the continual and endless discursiveness in our mind. All that discursiveness—what does it do? Unchecked, unliberated, it weakens our windhorse. It dulls the ability to experience Ashe. It begins to play tricks on our view because it solidifies the illusion of "me."

Traditionally it is said that the view is like our eyes and meditation is like our legs. If we forget where we are going or why we want to go there, we stop walking. That's why our meditation will be successful only as long as we keep the view.

The warrior who is meek has the view of discernment, like a tiger walking slowly through the jungle. Discernment—in Tibetan, *payu*—is knowing how to work with the mind. If we are able to see what to cultivate and what to discard—even as we work with our own thought patterns—then we are raising personal drala.

As warriors meditating properly, we are practicing the basis for the foundation for the kingdom of Shambhala. We are practicing the ability to see our own aggression and how it creates the kingdom of fear, the kingdom of self, the kingdom of animosity towards others. As warriors we are saying, "That is not the kingdom I am living in. Because I have planted the genuine Ashe in my mind stream, I can radiate another kind of energy."

The more we trust this practice, the more we see that it really works. It is very, very potent. Thanks to the blessings of the lineage of practitioners and great warriors before us who have instructed us to trust this situation, we can generate tremendous confidence. We can expand the energy of the Ashe outward and watch our thoughts lean over like grass being blown by the wind. Once we have confidence in our understanding of the nature of thoughts, they are easier and easier to disperse. The result of dispersing them is complete friendliness, peace, and harmony. Friendship means there is lack of agitation. We are no longer creating tension.

MERCY

Then we have the next step—being merciful to others. Mercy is having enough friendliness with our own mind to see someone else's predicament. It comes from knowing what happens if we do not have mercy. To act without mercy is to act from the outlook of the setting sun, which means acting with aggression.

According to the teachings, one moment of anger destroys aeons of practice. Aggression is like a spear that deflates windhorse and lungta. In the Shambhala teachings we learn that the natural response to any situation is gentleness and mercy. That is how we release ourselves from the fetters of aggression. When we act that way, we are acting mercifully toward others.

We know that the best thing to do right now is to be merciful, because if we engage differently we are denigrating our own windhorse. In doing so we will leave the family of the Rigden and sink into the lower realms. In that moment when we do not act in a merciful way, when for a split second we fail to trust the genuine Ashe, that's what happens. So one aspect of meek is that the warrior is very pragmatic.

ONE-POINTEDNESS

Another aspect of meek is that the warrior's mind is not stolen by ordinary activities. What do we mean by ordinary activities? In the traditional language of shamatha, *tse-chik* means one-pointedness. A one-pointed mind does not wander. The warrior does not lose dignity by engaging in ordinary, seemingly inconsequential activities of the mind.

An example of ordinary and meaningless activity is self-perpetuating doubt that the path is worthy. With the dignity of meek we will be able to discern what we are up to and stop putting our mind on the treadmill of this particular form of entertainment. We will begin to see that ordinary activities and our fascination with them are a symptom of boredom. Boredom is the symptom of not understanding our own potential. Instead, we are preoccupied by habitual tendencies. The result is that we live our lives in a discursive way.

With discernment, we begin to know when we smell bad because we did certain things or acted in certain ways that were degrading to others and ourselves. At these times, having slipped into ordinariness, our mind has taken us in a particular direction. As a result we now have to deal with overcoming our kleshas, cleaning up what we should have discarded and beginning to cultivate what we should have been cultivating all along. Recognizing this warrior mind as the most precious mind, we should continuously engage it with acts of virtue.

NOWNESS

We have been given the teachings on the present—nowness—in Sanskrit, *tathata*. When we are completely present, past and future don't exist. We are not thinking about what we could do in the future, we are not rehashing what happened in the past, we are acting now. Whether it is from an inner point of view of our own meditation or from an outer point of view of participating in an organization, creating the kingdom of Shambhala is very much about dealing with right now. The teachings of nowness and the present moment are always occurring.

When we live in a mind that is perpetually fooled by time, we think there is going to be a better time. Whenever that better time comes along, we are unable to act because we have not clarified our mind. We have not raised our windhorse, so when that next moment comes, we can't pounce. This is why we need to be exerting ourselves, practicing constantly.

When warriors of meek live in an unselfish way, sacredness begins to shine through the world as the complete yün of the Rigden fathers. Our senses—taste, touch, sight, smell, sound—take on a richer quality, with a strong sense of appreciation. Having learned to engage in mindfulness, we are no longer struggling. There is space in the mind and we are able to appreciate the simplicity and satisfaction of being meek. Then we can accomplish our activity fluidly, with ease.

THE LAW OF KARMA

The warrior who is meek knows that the reason we habitually engage in life in a fearful way is related with the accumulation of previous actions. Whether we did something in a virtuous or nonvirtuous way is revealing itself right now. As warriors we look at our minds, take control, and tame the situation in order to go forward. The key to this approach is discernment. If we are not discerning and become subjugated by anger or speed, we will pay the price later.

The practice of meekness is a process of appreciation, humbleness, and not being fooled. We are no longer fooled into thinking we can handle what we can't. We respect karma—causes and conditions. Karma is not particularly a Buddhist term—it is a worldly term, a truth that anyone can observe: the process of things coming together and having a particular repercussion. The Buddha said that the law of karma does not guarantee that certain things will happen. If we infuse past karma with virtuous karma now, we can change the course of our life in any direction we want and at any particular point along the way. Either this is true, or the Buddha is wrong. Beginning to see that it is possible will give us the confidence to change our lives by cultivating virtue.

Meekness is very intelligent. It is a process of overcoming hope and fear, those elements that create the dilemma of desperately wanting something to happen, which takes us into the lower realms. We want something to happen, and that is hope. We're afraid it won't happen, and that is fear. Because we do not know what to cultivate and what to discard, we are hoping for the best and fearing the worst. Hope and fear are mired in ignorance and bewilderment. In practicing meekness we see that hope comes from fear—not knowing what is going to happen. This is life—there's no way to know exactly what is going to happen. We can only understand where we're at and what we can do.

In the vajrayana when we talk about crazy wisdom, we often invoke Padmasambhava's statement, "My mind is like the sky, and my actions are like a sesame seed." That doesn't mean, "My actions are like the sky, I can do whatever I want and my mind hopefully is not like a sesame seed." It means that on the most minute level, I know what I am doing. I am discerning. I consider my actions carefully because I respect karma. Padmasambhava himself—the *tertön* who buried teachings in the realm of the secret court, to be discovered later by the Dorje Dradül—says, "We have to respect karma." Incidentally, we can regard Padmasambhava as Shambhalian because he was both a Buddhist teacher and a worldly king.

DOT AS VIEW/STROKE AS MEDITATION

As warriors of meek, to respect karma does not mean that we are afraid. It means that we have our senses open and we know what we are engaging in. This process begins in meditation. Sometimes we think of meditation as a sunbathing session: we sit and catch the rays for a while and then it's time to go back to work. Instead we should be regarding our meditation as training. We place the dot, which is view, and do the stroke, which is the meditation, diligently and loosely, combining these. As we relax our mind within the discipline, we become gentler and stronger, gaining tremendous energy. That is how we use the Ashe as training for warriorship.

Having practiced in the comfort of our own meditation, we can experiment with taking these teachings out into the world. It is important to know how much we can take on— what is enough and what is too much. At times we need to develop our energy, at others we need to balance our energy, and sometimes we need to protect our energy. There are times when we're challenged, but we can handle it. At other times we're losing momentum, so we need to back off. That's not being self-centered; it is being meek. If we try too hard when we're weak, our energy just gets consumed. These teachings are trying to make us strong.

When we're strong, the Ashe will naturally radiate out; it won't be a thought process. But first we need to be meek. Tiger, lion, garuda, and dragon are stages we go through, from working with mindfulness and contentment, to developing certainty in compassion, to working with not separating the world between friends and enemies. These stages are interdependent. Meekness is the seed for the perkiness of the lion, the outrageousness of the garuda, and the inscrutability of the dragon. Without the practice of meekness, outrageousness and inscrutability will not happen.

10

THE DIGNITY OF PERKY

DISCIPLINE: THE FOUR-LEGGED MIRACLE OF WINDHORSE

Perky means knowing what to do, because now we understand that virtue leads to happiness. The main aspect of virtue is benefiting others. The Dorje Dradül said that the Shambhala warrior gladly goes on the path of virtue, which is the four-legged miracle of windhorse—aspiration, exertion, stable mind, and virtuous activity.

Meek has laid the ground, and now we are talking about doubtlessness—being certain about what kind of actions lead us towards awakening. The warrior of perky has discipline. With discipline we know how to move ourselves in the right direction because we understand what we're doing. Discipline is a very good word, because discipline brings joy.

Most of us might know generally what to cultivate, but we have a hard time knowing specifically how to move forward. Specifically, we need to know how to raise windhorse in a

continuous way, how to purify ourselves so that we smell better to others and to ourselves. We need to awaken our prajna,
the critical intelligence that begins to see the nature of every
situation. When we are enticed with an invitation to do something questionable, we need to remember the path of golden
virtue.

The image of perky is the snow lion. It is said that the snow
lion lives in the highland meadows. In the flag of Tibet snow
lions are holding up the sun. In lama dancing, the snow lion
bounces around with discipline and joy.

FLIPPING THOUGHTS OUTWARDLY

To develop the qualities of a snow lion, we cultivate compassion by contemplating it. Contemplation is the actual
experience of sifting through our thoughts and prioritizing
which one goes first, which one goes second. That is applying wisdom. I've noticed that when I am overly worried about
something, I can flip my attitude by generating a mind of
compassion, thinking about others instead of giving in to my
own frustration. Flipping thoughts outwardly toward people
in need relaxes the mind, which allows delight to arise. When
it is delighted, the mind becomes light.

The snow lion symbolizes that nimbleness. It's the feeling
we have when we do something nice for someone else, like
preparing a meal. Likewise, if someone does something nice
for us, we remember it all day. We recognize virtue when we
see it. Our sense of delight is a simple reflection that we are
leading our life according to that principle.

When I think about the lightness that comes from acting virtuously, I often recall my teachers. As they grow older, they become more and more cheerful. If I ask them how they manage to have that level of happiness, they reply that it comes from turning the mind towards others. Turning the mind towards others might sound like a lot of work, but it requires much more effort and energy to think about ourselves. That is truly high maintenance.

Because the discipline of perky begins to dissolve the dualism of "me" and "you," the mind can finally play. We are no longer hindering its natural tendency to extend itself because we are no longer fooled by the seeming solidity of appearances. We are moving forward; we are no longer confused about what is genuine and what is not, about what is good and what is bad. We no longer doubt our nature, and we naturally extend compassion to others. The snow lion jumps from mountaintop to mountaintop because it has been completely liberated through certainty in its natural energy.

DOUBTLESSNESS FEELS GOOD

The energy of perky comes from knowing on a deep inner level that we are doing the right thing. We have wandered in discursiveness, we have tried other methods, and now we're on a path that is leading somewhere. Of course, we have to temper our excitement with discipline. That is how we achieve the higher realms, where the mind and body get clearer. Our experience of the world becomes more youthful. There's a sense of buoyancy, the result of meek and perky.

That joy purifies and rarifies the density of our mind so that it is more porous—the better for the Great Eastern Sun to shine through. This translucence comes from knowing what to do, which way to go. We know how to act, so doubtlessness feels good.

When we fall into the trap of doubt, the dralas will appear. They can be friendly or pesky. If we do not pay attention to the dralas, we will fall down to the lower realms much more quickly than an ordinary person. We have been given a gift— beginning to divide it up and not trust it causes further doubt and we sink fast. If we want to be happy, even on a worldly level, we must help others. If the mind extends at all that way, immediately we are benefiting others, and simultaneously whatever we want gets accomplished, because our windhorse increases.

11

THE DIGNITY OF OUTRAGEOUS

SPONTANEITY FULL-BLOWN

Tiger and lion are the earth, the proper ground from which to pounce and jump. When we get to outrageous and inscrutable, we are entering a more transcendent level—a fathomless, nonconceptual level.

It is said that suffering and pain arise because we separate ourselves from other beings. When we contemplate compassion, we begin to realize that we aren't separated from others at all: they are having the same experiences that we are, because we all want happiness. None of us wants suffering. As this insight deepens, the boundary between "us" and "them" begins to melt. This melting quality is symbolized by the garuda.

The garuda is born from an egg full-grown. It is said that the egg sat there for something like five hundred years, and finally the garuda popped out, able to function completely.

According to the dzokchen tradition, the garuda's full-blown quality represents *lhündrup* and *yeshe*, which means spontaneous wisdom—the complete actualization, embodiment, and boundless play of wisdom itself. Its wings represent prajna—"best knowledge"—and *upaya*—"skillful means"—and it holds a snake, which symbolizes transforming poison into amrita, nectar.

Because of its clear vision, the garuda is known for being able to overcome obstacles and diseases. The most serious obstacle is not trusting in our awakened quality. Out of that lack of trust comes ignorance, and out of ignorance come kleshas, which produce harmful acts. Since most physical illnesses are considered to be a result of previous negative actions, this disease of the mind is the root disease.

The tiger's energy of meek is oriented toward developing virtue and abandoning nonvirtue. The lion's energy of perky is oriented toward accomplishing compassion and doubt-lessness. With the garuda's outrageous quality of space and wisdom, we are so confident in the nature of our mind that we abandon all conceptual polarities. We abandon hope; we abandon fear; we abandon discarding, incorporating, and accomplishing. The space we find is without cause, a self-existing confidence very much related to meditation.

There are practices in which we meditate on the garuda and extend our consciousness into space with the confidence that is fearless in the vast sky of our impartial mind. We are not afraid to poke and prod all of mind's dimensions, because we understand that we are complete, perfect, and intact, and that we were born that way, like the garuda. As *The Letter of the Black Ashe* says, our mind is "A good self-existing sword: Desire to sharpen it will make it dull."

EXPERIENCING EQUANIMITY

Much of our lives we are seeking comfort, trying to take the edge off our experience by pampering ourselves. Engaging with our own lungta makes us able and tough. One of the most important qualities we can cultivate in this process is equanimity. Most of us are always struggling with our mind. It's as if we think we won't suffer if we keep things churning. With equanimity, we can let it be. We can give it a break. When we let go, the mind relaxes. That is the dignity of the garuda.

Getting upset when somebody takes something away from us or hurts us demonstrates that we don't have equanimity. We don't really understand how our mind works. We think that our mind is real and that something is happening to us. We don't appreciate the dralas of richness. The world is continuously rich. Whether we seemingly lose or gain something does not matter. We can see this in the lives of great warriors.

In a sense, we are talking about the difference between the dead world and the awakened world. The dead world is conditioned—it came from somewhere, it is going somewhere, and something is going to be taken away. The awakened world is beginningless and endless. There is nothing to be taken away. To have equanimity is not to ignore or pretend, but to reflect this reality with the mind. With the mind of the garuda, we transcend the tendency to divide the world up into categories like ugly or pretty, sweet or sour. The practices of the warrior are able to cut through those projections.

Once we understand the nature of phenomena, we see the purity and equality of all things. We have foresight; we see what is going on in the bigger picture, because we sense the real vastness of the Great Eastern Sun. With that kind of big mind and inner brilliance, the warrior shines forth in the world.

We might think, "At the end I want to be enlightened, but I still want to be me so that I can enjoy it. I'd like to have that wisdom and intensity, but if I change too much, I won't really be me anymore." The point of warriorship is that there is a transformation. We are going to be changed dramatically— hopefully for the better. We are challenged to do this in every moment by letting go, letting go, and letting go.

In terms of the energy he brought to the West, the Dorje Dradül himself went through a transformation when he decided to present the Shambhala teachings. He decided to manifest as Sakyong, presenting particular teachings in a particular language for the benefit of beings at this specific time. As he used to say himself, otherwise he would have been just a nice Tibetan chap rather than the great leader that he was.

Just like the Dorje Dradül thrust into a new world, whether or not he expected it, we cannot hold time still, for it is moving anyway. Change is one of the main characteristics of karma. If we are engaged in karma, we are engaged in change. In order to understand time and change, we are fortunate to have the Shambhala dharma. With clear vision, a big view, and the weaponry of confidence, we engage in life with a quality of knowing what we are doing—because we're awake.

HONING THE ASHE

Yet mostly when we engage in life there are many areas that we do not know, and therefore we divide life into eternalism and nihilism—hope and fear. We perpetually go from one extreme to the other. The Great Eastern Sun has at its core the ability to transcend the dynamic of hope and fear in a non-conceptual way. Within a nuclear force in the middle of the Great Eastern Sun its principles are radiating out, manifesting as sacred world. Thus the way of the Great Eastern Sun is the middle way, free from extremes.

How do we go beyond hope and fear? The relative Ashe has to be honed and sharpened against our experience, day by day. Does that mean that the Ashe is getting sharper? No, it means our ability to trust the Ashe, our ability to act with the Ashe—to penetrate concept and recognize the genuine—is getting sharper. Within that moment of being awake and clear, we also have a tremendous sense of intelligence. That is real lungta, knowing our own nature and resting there.

We sometimes talk about the phenomenon of prajna as opposed to the sword of prajna. The phenomenon of prajna means that the world itself becomes a sharpening stone for the relative Ashe. When the phenomenal world presents itself, we are able to engage in it mercifully. Every time we act in a merciful way, we gain more confidence. When we do not trust the relative Ashe, we act in an aggressive way, which dulls it. That diminishes our confidence, reducing our ability to lay the ground for further confidence.

Honing the Ashe comes down to looking at what is happening now—not in the future, not in the past. The warriors of the lineage have said, "Act in this way," and therefore what will happen? The golden age of Shambhala will dawn, and we will recognize the nature of our mind as basic goodness. At some point we will be able to look at even the most ordinary situation and regard it as golden. Our windhorse will be strong enough to break through.

But it won't be strong enough to keep us on that spot for long; we'll be able to see sacred world only for a snap second. We will see the notion of secret court—no center and no fringe. We will see that the concept of fringe and center is completely fabricated. When we see this, we won't lose our seat, we won't freak out, we won't be fearful. Beginning to get a taste of this energy reinforces the direction we're going, which beings tremendous joy. Our windhorse rises. We feel uplifted by our natural ziji. This is complete simplicity. The Great Eastern Sun is shining, illuminating darkness. Wherever there is not-knowing, it shines and it knows. Therefore the mind is naked, unhindered, and free.

12

THE DIGNITY OF INSCRUTABLE

NONCONCEPTUAL REALITY

The Letter of the Black Ashe says that the mind of the inscrutable warrior is "like space which cannot be punctured by an arrow." That means there are no weak spots in the meditation. Our meditative mind doesn't dissipate, because our perceptions are engaged in the sacredness of ordinary phenomena.

Sacredness means having intelligence. Wherever we are, no matter what we are doing, we can see that tangible energy of the Rigden—enlightenment, complete freedom, beginningless and endless. We no longer fear interruption or distraction. It is not that we can stare so well that we blanket everything with our wishful thinking. Rather, the mind has now developed the ability to completely cut and penetrate. We are taking refuge in the pure appearance of how things are.

The stage of practice at which the final conceptual barrier begins to dissolve is known as dragon. That barrier is the sense of self that we have continuously carried with us. We've been pretending that something that is not there is there, like believing in a mirage. The confidence of the dragon embodies tremendous fluidity because we are no longer preoccupied with such illusions.

The dragon symbolizes wisdom. It lives high in the sky, reflecting the quality of space and realization that are possible only when we have overcome the claustrophobia of "me." When this happens we become inscrutable, with wisdom that cannot be torn, punctured, or diminished. We never know what an individual with a nonconceptual mind is thinking. We never know what he or she is doing. We can only guess at what is happening.

It is said that we experience the mind of inscrutability when we are sitting in meditation with the Ashe descending. Because of meek, we visualize it correctly; because of perky, we rest in it and experience a sense of joy—we know we are doing the right thing. Outrageous is having confidence in the Ashe and expanding out so we relax our mind in space. Inscrutable is being fearless and having confidence that any alteration of the mind will not affect its nature. When we plant the Ashe in our heart, we are liberating our mind into nonconceptuality. The energy of the Rigden is present and engaged.

ABANDONING SPIRITUALITY AND MATERIALISM

When the Ashe sits there naturally in our heart, we relax and gaze out, extending our mind from that critical intelligence, prajna. This intelligence is innate in the Ashe, which cuts concept without hesitation. We have to relax totally in order to access this critical mind, but that doesn't mean just sinking in a blasé way; the mind is totally engaged. It is critical because it is courageous and willing to really look at our perceptions. This critical intelligence dissolves our misperceptions.

With that confidence and warriorship, we now know our own senses, untainted by conceptual mind. The world as we have always perceived it dissolves. Every bite we take does not immediately bring up "tastes good" or "tastes bad." Perceiving in this relaxed and penetrating way is very much the experience of windhorse. Our mind and its perception of the world are without fetter.

Usually our perceptions are impeded. When we're looking at someone, our eyes stop at their face or their clothing; we cannot perceive their mind. Since that's our habit, we don't think we have the ability to perceive more deeply. Sometimes when we come out of a long practice period we find ourselves so relaxed that when we look at somebody we see much more than we did before. It isn't that the other person became more open, but that we are more able to look and see what is really there. This happens because we are no longer a nuisance to ourselves. Because we have drala—conviction in our knowledge of basic goodness—our confidence is not threatened by someone else's presence. There is nothing of ours that they can get and there is nothing of theirs for us to want, so our gain-and-victory mentality, which involves constant ups and downs, is gone.

The warrior of inscrutable is all-victorious, temporally and spiritually: the things to accumulate—which sometimes refer to materialism—and the things to accept or abandon—which sometimes refer to spirituality—have all been completely conquered. Resting in this way, behaving in this way, and understanding in this way increase our ability to use everyday experience to sharpen the Ashe in our heart.

At that level of confidence we are resting more nakedly and simply, with increased authentic presence. Sitting in that completely relaxed mode, we are universal monarchs. This is where spiritual and temporal come together. There is no split, because the nature of the mind, what the mind can do, and how the warrior proceeds have transcended duality. This is how the Rigden manifests.

RIGDEN AS ULTIMATE DRALA

The Rigden represents the ultimate drala. It is our own nature. At its essence Rigden is complete primordialness, which means that it is beyond mind. Primordialness is unconditioned, free from causes and conditions. In Tibetan we say *sem-le depa*—beyond the ability to grasp. The guardian of that particular state of mind is the *she*, the ability to cut nonliberated mind.

The Rigden has no beginning. That beginningless quality means that there is no birth. Birth creates the scenario where we experience a level of duality and suffering, so obviously the Rigden has transcended this situation. There is no creator; therefore the Rigden is not created. The Rigden is not a thing; it is not an individual; it is not a self. It is complete egolessness.

The Rigden has discovered his own basic goodness and therefore, without any pretense and with no journey necessary, the ultimate enthronement has occurred instantaneously. That is celestial appointment, innate rulership. The Rigden is the king of kings who can join heaven and earth inseparably and perfectly, which means joining mind and body. Joining mind and body creates action.

CREATING THE PALACE OF THE RIGDENS

Action is regarded as temporal involvement—what the Dorje Dradül called livelihood. When we join mind and body— meaning that we understand our nature—we are humble, we have incredible inscrutability, we are not beguiled into misperception, and we know the meditative mind. Therefore we are buoyant and free. When we have that direct connection with the world, we ourselves are a king or queen in the best sense of the word. Those are the qualities of rulership on this level, and that is why the Rigden is considered to be a sacred king— a *chögyal*, or dharma king. Dharma means truth.

We pay homage to great rulers such as Gesar of Ling, Prince Shotoku, Emperor Yung Lo, and Ashoka because they had the confidence to create Shambhala vision. It has to do with the notion of relative court, or outer court. Having confidence and courage that we are going to create the palace of the Rigdens in our own environment, we can take the attitude, "Here I am, and I know for sure the power of sacredness. This little house can be the manifestation of that principle." We begin to see our environment with king's view, the perspective of the Rigden.

In our lineage, the Sakyong represents and embodies that blessing. The Sakyong is the venue by which we are able to access the ability to hold court in our own domain. When we use heavy words like "court" and talk about its exterior and interior aspects, we need to remember that at the ultimate level, the secret level, there is no exterior or interior. It is primordial, nonconceptual, and fathomless. Like the Rigden king, it does not have to be created; otherwise it would have to cease. Not only is it all-accomplishing, there is also incredible profundity and depth. When our mind begins to slow down, it's as if we've poked a hole in the dam and the truth comes gushing out. Day after day we open our mind and more and more truth comes out. That is the notion of profundity.

The truth is profound because it is inconceivable. We can't understand it by poking it once and moving on to the next thing. We have to keep circling around it. Our minds generally exist in terms of time. We have a beginning thought and an end thought. Within the process, we even want to think about what we have thought before it diminishes, and we want to hold on to what we are about to think before we have thought it. The inscrutable wisdom of the dragon is beyond those concepts. It is beyond time. It sustains itself. It is almost like a feeling. It is very, very profound.

13

WINDHORSE AND THE
BREEZE OF DELIGHT

JUST THE WAY IT IS

When we raise windhorse, like a cool breeze Ashe opens the
door of our self-induced claustrophobia. The result is humor, a
natural response that implies both intelligence and relaxation.
Now that our mind is Ashe, we can laugh at ourselves. Why
are we amused? We are amused by how we have been fooled.

It's like looking back after an argument and saying, "How
ridiculous. I can't believe how upset I was." We had to let some
time pass before we could see clearly. There may be a sense of
embarrassment when we see that we actually hung on to the
last donut and didn't want to give it to anybody else. We don't
want to tell somebody that we cut off an old lady in the gro-
cery line because we were in a rush and had only two items,
and she had a lot of stuff. We feel embarrassed about looking for logical explanations for our subhuman behavior. We
see that we don't want to live this way. We're always going to

have to buy groceries, and there is probably always going to be somebody in the line ahead. That's life; it's just the way it is. Arranging our life to be one convenient situation after another for the benefit of "me" is entrapment in fear and depression. In that case we're going to feel bad about everything. We see now that we can raise windhorse with the attitude, "Now that I am a Shambhala citizen, I take a different view. I am leading a sacred life on a temporal level, where I believe in the basic goodness of all beings. That woman in front of me could have been the Rigden king—how am I to know?"

Looking at the world from the perspective of basic goodness is how we realize the kingdom of Shambhala in our everyday situation. Ashe practice is a way of recognizing our family lineage, our sense of warriorship, and rising to it. That is what we are trying to inspire ourselves to do. There will be situations where we forget about that and feel embarrassed about the results. Depending on our perception, the path will be bumpy or smooth.

Our attitude in raising windhorse accounts for the difference. The more we trust Ashe, the more playful our mind will be. We can stand in line completely delighted to see what the old lady ahead is buying, or we can shut the door on the whole situation and watch our mind move on to what we think is meaningful. We could say there is a certain basic intelligence in moving on, but that isn't true: in that case we are still running from our mind in order to seemingly enjoy ourselves. Once we get to the next situation, the speed of mind that closed the door on that old lady shows up and we're not able to enjoy our drink or our pretzels. We get an upset stomach. This is just an example. The point is that when we trust the Ashe, we have a sense of humor.

WHY ARE THE DRALAS HAPPY?

The humor comes from a genuine source, a liberated source —seeing *now* as an opportunity to practice. We can even feel amused when we see how we have missed that opportunity. We feel further amused when we realize who is having the biggest laugh of all—the dralas. The Rigden king, the Rigden queen, Shiwa Ökar, and the whole gang are yukking it up because they are jumping up and down right in front of us, saying, "Here we are! Here we are!" while we're sitting here so seriously, not trusting the Ashe.

Why are the Rigdens happy? They are laughing because they see how utterly close we are to enlightenment. They know we are just a few steps from the top of the mountain, and they know what it takes to get there. They are totally delighted by our exertion, discipline, meditation, patience, generosity, and prajna. They are happy to receive us. Once we trust the Ashe, we begin to enjoy the show.

This breeze of delight is a result of windhorse. We are over-coming our own ambition, aggression, and fear. Before, even mentioning those words brought on a rush of bad associa-tions. Now we can laugh in the face of it. When we mix that humor with critical intelligence, we have wisdom, the embodi-ment of the Great Eastern Sun.

RIDING THE WIND

Consciousness is all over the body in the form of wind. When we raise lungta, we are dealing with that wind. We are bringing the energy in and cutting our habitual tendencies, the notion of self or ego.

Sometimes when we're sitting, we say, "My mind feels thick." Well, it is thick—very thick. It has been thick for a long time and that is why it feels thick now. Unfortunately, it may feel thick tomorrow. We cannot think that we have this corporeal body and are therefore stupid and lazy and that's just how it is. We have to begin to look at the teachings on egolessness and realize that there is nobody here—it is just an appearance. There is a concept of self, and the warrior's challenge is not to be deluded by it.

By visualizing the Ashe, we are reminding ourselves of who we are. Understanding the nature of our mind, we are purifying our mind stream and strengthening our *lung*—life force. By doing this we can change the karmic conditions of this particular lifetime, which leads to living longer or living in a more healthy manifestation.

Many years ago, my mother requested a divination from a renowned Tibetan oracle, a man who, much like the Dorje Dradül, could look into a mirror and see different levels of reality. Even lamas in India send requests to him because his readings are very clear. Relaying a message through one of her relatives in Tibet, my mother asked about her own and the rest of the family's health. This was in 1987. The oracle invoked Gesar of Ling and told her that karmically speaking, her life was to last only so many years, but because of her strong windhorse, she would live longer. That is very much what we are talking about.

Windhorse is the vehicle on which our consciousness rides. It purifies our mind stream, thinning the density of the habitual tendencies. The tradition of windhorse and what we are trying to do on an inner level is represented by the process of purification that happens through the smoke of the *lhasang*. In that ceremony we raise windhorse: the smoke goes up, and the dralas come down. In the same way, the Ashe descends through our consciousness, resting in our heart center.

It is very important to remember that Ashe is a worldly manifestation, a worldly practice. The key element is our certainty in the nature of reality, basic goodness. It is said that the individual who manifests with the confidence of a warrior looks and smells different from other people. It is almost as if a physiological change occurs. That is the potency of windhorse—trust in the relative Ashe.

Whether we are in a higher realm or a lower one, we always have relative Ashe. The path of the four dignities strengthens our conviction in it. Meek, perky, outrageous, and inscrutable are ways of describing the process of becoming a full human being. Each of the four dignities is a further empowerment to recognize and trust the relative Ashe. Each dignity is a way of saying, "I am a warrior."

As warriors, we should respect that everybody is included within the kingdom of Shambhala because we all have that relative Ashe sitting in our heart—tapped or untapped. Whether or not we know it, we all have mercy and wisdom. We need to awaken it. To criticize other lineages or religious traditions is actually breaking our vow. Any kind of slight reduces our ability to accomplish liberation. Windhorse is everywhere and anyone can raise it; we are not necessarily an elite group of individuals. However, because we have been given this particular transmission and encouragement, we can raise windhorse now.

14

COURT PRINCIPLE AND SACRED WORLD

KALAPA

As we read in *The Golden Sun of the Great East,* there is a historical moment where Dawa Sangpo proclaims the Ashe, expressing the truth and thereby subjugating the evil forces. He is surrounded by the father lineage and the mother lineage—representing the dralas—and the lineage of ministers and *dapöns,* representing the protectors. It is said that we need these elements to establish a good human society. We need them to understand and experience the Great Eastern Sun. By bringing them together, we can actually accomplish these things.

This is the principle of court, which is related to the *mandala* principle. Without it, the direct transmission and the genuine confidence will not be planted in us properly. Thus we will always have doubt that the teachings can be accomplished; we will doubt that we can do it. So traditionally speaking, when we are talking about very profound teachings that have to do with the nature of mind, such as Ashe, it is important to create a mandala.

The mandala of Shambhala is called the court. It shows us how to regard our inner body, our physical body, and phenomena as a display of sacred world. The court of Shambhala is the radiant manifestation of the Primordial Rigden. It is called Kalapa, the palace of the Rigdens. "Profound, brilliant, just, powerful, all-victorious" are the qualities of the Rigdens and of a Shambhala person. There are secret, inner, and outer aspects.

The secret, or ultimate, aspect of the court is related to "profound." It is embodied by the Primordial Rigden abiding in the cosmic mirror. The Rigden is unchanging and has a quality of great ziji. The secret court is pristine, unequivocal, and brilliant with the radiance of the Great Eastern Sun. It has no boundaries, no beginning, and no end. The drala of that situation is the absolute Ashe.

When we think about what absolute is, or what Great Eastern Sun is, our mind wants to put it in terms of center and fringe. We want to ask, "Which part is compassion, which part is brilliance, which part is beginning, which part is end?" We want someone else to tell us what is what. The absolute Ashe, the drala of the ultimate court, says, "That is not going to work. You have to take the whole thing at once." The drala is the protector of nonconceptual truth. We cannot approach our mind through the gates of the absolute and say, "Please let me in." We have to be able to release ourselves from concep-

tual mind. At the moment when we actually release, we enter
into the absolute Ashe, which is the basis of everything.

To enter the secret court is to be able to recognize the genuine. The ultimate court has no fringe, no center. It is neither
eternalistic nor nihilistic. To have confidence is a process
of being able to naturally recognize these qualities with our
heart.

The inner court aspect is related to "brilliant" and is embodied by werma and drala, the mother and father lineages and
the other ancestral lineages, all radiating the Great Eastern
Sun. That wisdom shines forth because its base is eternal,
before thought, and unconditioned. It has no hope and no fear
and is beyond the limits and confines of accepting and rejecting.

As the manifestation of this inherent, complete luminosity,
the inhabitants of the inner court are fearless. Because they
are beyond accepting or rejecting, they are constantly available and helping all beings. Their qualities include the gentleness of the mother lineage, the fearlessness of the father
lineage, and the prajna that they both hold, produced by lack
of aggression.

The outer aspect is related to "just" and "powerful." As the
Dorje Dradül has said, the outer court cannot be penetrated
because it has a protection of sanity. Confusion cannot enter
and therefore it radiates the Great Eastern Sun.

The outer court is inhabited by the Sakyong and Sakyong
Wangmo. Because their minds are steeped in true and genuine
windhorse and authentic presence, they have an indestructible
quality, embodying the qualities of the perfect warrior—skill,

daring, and patience. The six ways of ruling are part of their skillfulness, with the first three—benevolent, true, genuine—related to being just, and the last three—fearless, artful, and rejoicing—related to being powerful. Being just and powerful is how the warrior manifests in the world.

THE SIX WAYS OF RULING

JUST

"Just" has to do with our own conviction: we are *benevolent*, *true*, and *genuine*. Being *benevolent* is related to patience. As warriors, we can't just push things through; we must engage our world with a sense of not being in a rush with our own mind. We're not trying to force people to do things that they can't do. We're not trying to get projects going prematurely. We are patient and benevolent.

The next way of ruling is to be *true*. Being true is being steadfast. We don't flip-flop, saying one thing one day and something else the next. Instead of changing our minds all the time, we cultivate a sense of steadiness. Patience helps us do that, with the result that we know what direction we want to go. Being true connotes a level of integrity.

The third way of ruling is being *genuine*. To be genuine is to be able to self-reflect, to know what is in your own mind and heart and not be afraid of it. Being genuine means knowing the right thing to do: you can genuinely be late and you can genuinely be early. You can genuinely make mistakes. However, if you are not genuine, it's very hard to find yourself because there are so many layers on top. When you are genuine, you don't need to try to impress others or try to fool others. Sometimes genuineness can be intimidating to others, because it reveals their nongenuineness; they would like you to play along.

Powerful

The next three ways of ruling—*fearless*, *artful*, and *rejoicing*—are elements of being powerful. They concern how we manifest outwardly, given our conviction in being benevolent, genuine, and true.

First, we are *fearless* in terms of how we would like to engage in our life. There's no second-guessing taking place; we are ready to go forward. If we're scared of our own power—indecisive and fearful—then we create fear, indecision, and confusion in those around us. With fearlessness, at some point we simply say "yes" or "no"—"maybe" goes out the door.

Being *artful* has a quality of timing. We're trying to conduct our life in a dignified way.

Rejoicing is the process of looking at what we have accomplished. Whether it's at the end of the day, the end of a project, or the end of our life, we feel a sense of appreciation. Our life has a natural meter, a pace. We stop to smell the roses. That sense of rejoicing uplifts those around us; without it our life becomes a grinding stone.

The six ways of ruling are skillful means. We are talking about the notion of being a good warrior, being genuine and courageous, which means we are daring to come out of our habitual patterns. As the Dorje Dradül liked to point out, it's hard to change habits incrementally; at a certain point, we need to come out of our habituation—mentally and physically—to take that courageous leap, and be daring. Once we are daring, the next step is to be more patient—not being so naively hopeful about our daring leap.

COURT PRINCIPLE IN DAILY LIFE

In talking about court principle, we are talking about our lives, in which all of us are kings or queens. We are trying to balance a life in which we have as guiding principles the masculine and the feminine principles, the protector principle, and the drala principle. We are trying to emulate the mandala principle; we are almost doing a sacred dance. In a lama dance, we might see the full display of Padmasambhava's court or the dharma king Trisong Detsen's court. That is a display of how enlightenment can manifest. Everybody within the dance visualizes themselves a certain way; they have a particular role to perform in the overall situation.

We use court principle in arranging the three palaces of our lives. The outer palace is the environment, the inner palace is the body, and the secret palace is the mind. We magnetize the blessing of drala by organizing these palaces properly. In terms of the outer palace, we arrange our environment to reflect the openness and precision of our mind.

In terms of the inner palace, we pay attention to how we use our mouth, moderating both what goes into it and what comes out of it. Each day we eat well, sleep well, take care of our bodies, and meditate—activities known in Tibet as the "four exhilarations" because they synchronize body and mind.

Moving our bodies with gentleness and precision—playing music or sports, dancing, or practicing martial arts—attracts drala. So does being attentive and appreciative when we prepare a meal, walk down the street, or drink a cup of tea. Wearing clothing that looks good and fits well draws drala down. We do this not to proclaim ourselves, but to invite the magic of each moment and through our presence, make it available to others.

In terms of the secret palace, drala is available to us only when we rise above aggression and attachment, expanding our perceptions. The dralas are attracted to virtue. *Dra* is enemy, *la* means above. By "above" we mean above nonvirtue.

It is said that the difference between enlightened society and a degraded society lies in the ability of those individuals to see that genuine goodness does exist. It is connected to the individuals' realization, a subjective way of looking at the world. It is a way of understanding how things are and seeing the goodness in it. The way we do that is to have courage to think, "I can do it." The moment we think "I can do it" is a decisive moment. It is Ashe, the drala of confidence coming through. The more that drala comes up, the more we will see, hear, and know the right thing to do. With the practice of Ashe, we are empowering ourselves with this point of view.

IV
ACTING OUT REALITY

15

GUIDED MEDITATION: RAISING WINDHORSE

Before we begin, we say to ourselves, "I am taking this posture; I am meditating. The Great Eastern Sun in my heart is the subject. The object is Ashe, the ground nature." As we look up, we have the confidence that through proper meditation, we will get a glimpse of this.

Great Eastern Sun is the great gift within. It is our ability to give birth and recognize wisdom in ourselves. We have within our own mind and heart a wisdom that primordially has never been confused. When we're meditating, it is not another mind, it is not from somewhere else, it is this very mind that is fabricating everything. From within that mind we want to awaken. We want to understand Ashe. We want to understand that *A*. What is going to understand the *A*? The Great Eastern Sun. What has covered the *A*? Darkness and misunderstanding, the setting sun, barbarians—beings who have given up on confidence.

We can talk about the barbarians of the setting sun in terms of stress or depression—our mind gets heavy. We could say, "I just want to clear my mind." One way to do that is through shamatha, but we have to keep doing it again and again; that's the problem with shamatha. This is a better practice, the best practice, because we are bringing out our awakened nature on the spot.

A has the quality of that absolute nature, the ground nature, doma-ne sangpo, basic goodness. We want to reveal it; we want to bring that out. *She* is "let's do it." We can do it; we are going to do it; we have a method. The method of Ashe also relies on anatomy: within our heart center, Ashe is physically present.

When we're born we already have Ashe—undiluted, unobscured, perfect, intact wisdom—in our heart. Sometimes this Ashe is called the "innate lamp of prajna." Ashe is the ground, but it is the Great Eastern Sun that knows that the Ashe is there. That wisdom is what we have to awaken.

So first we take a good warrior posture, with our hands on the thighs. How we hold our body enables us to see wisdom or keeps us from seeing it, so the posture is important. Our gaze is going to be straight ahead, and the trunk is erect but not stiff.

We have many levels of thoughts and ideas, so now we relax our mind. Gradually we focus on the breathing, basic shamatha, exhaling and inhaling, exhaling and inhaling. We feel the rhythm of the breathing. That begins to ground us and calm us down. Having established a little bit of ground that way, we expand our mind out with the notion of vastness. To expand is to relax the mind, releasing it from conceptuality and hesitation. If we don't do that, expanding out becomes just another thought. We might think of expanding out in a physical sense, too. We can think, "I need to expand my mind out of the shrine tent into the buddha fields, all the way to town."

Now in front of us, off in the distance, a little bit high—but not too high—appears a black Ashe, a startling occurrence. We know that this is a direct transmission from the Rigdens, and we know what it means. *A* is the primordial quality, unbiased and unchanged, beyond good and bad. *She* is the notion of cutting. Ashe encapsulates our primordial enlightenment— the Great Eastern Sun—the wisdom and mercy that spans the three worlds. Intrinsically we know what that is.

We know now that this blackness is beyond relative truth. It is the ultimate nature. From this, everything comes about— birth, death, and everything in between. Yet mind itself is free from birth. So we contemplate that, which is in itself a profound exercise. The Ashe is like a diamond, brilliant, able to cut anything. It is fearlessness; nothing can destroy it. It is black-blue, and it begins to vibrate. The vibration is in a sense wrathful energy. This is not a stagnant practice.

As we hold our mind to the image, thoughts come and go, but we focus on the Ashe. It is the embodiment of all noble qualities; it has all the aspects of tiger, lion, garuda, and dragon. We're reaching in beyond time and space; it's the basis of all reality.

We are bringing the Ashe into our mind with the first two

aspects of visualization: clarity and pure recollection—seeing it clearly and recalling what it means. We are joining the image and its meaning through shamatha and vipashyana. Shamatha is holding the visualization. Vipashyana is knowing what the visualization means.

The third aspect of visualization is confidence, utter confidence that Ashe is the embodiment of our intrinsic nature. We understand that this is a meditation that will help us to understand what is already in our mind. In Ashe practice we are increasing our ability to touch into that ultimate nature and then act upon it.

We can talk about this in terms of *kyerim* and *dzogrim*, the generation and completion stages of practice. In kyerim we generate an image. There are many kinds of visualization practices in which we visualize images outside of us and then coming in, changing direction or movement. It's a dualistic approach, because we're focusing on something that's out there and bringing it in. The point is to be focused on the meaning of the symbol, and to use this method to incorporate the meaning. In this case we visualize the Ashe and begin to associate that image with reality, *chöying*, the space of phenomena. We realize that this space is vast, colorless, beyond manipulation. At the same time it is infused with great compassion.

The Ashe is like a fish vibrating, or like meteoric iron. Because of its cutting quality, it is also slightly wrathful. This sharp razor knife is coming at us. It has incredible prajna, ability to cut. As this seed syllable comes toward us and descends, it is a tremendous sense of energy, brilliance, and truth that dispels all our doubt and confusion. It melts these elements like the sun melting snow.

The Ashe is blazing with incredible wisdom; it is getting closer. Our mind may begin to wander, but we bring it back to the Ashe. We know that the shape itself is a transmission that has been given to us by the Dorje Dradül. If we were to ask him how we could experience his mind, he would say, "Visualize absolute reality in this format and you'll begin to get an idea."

At this point the Ashe is right in front of our forehead. Now it jumps into our body, which is empty like space, and at the same time, it flips. If somebody's looking at us, they'll see an Ashe in our head, which we do not visualize with the organs, but as a simple form. The Ashe is vibrating, radiating, beyond concept, beyond time. That intensity has never been denigrated.

As the Ashe descends from our head to our heart center, it rides on our mind stream, our lungta, our wind, our windhorse, which is in our body and mind, beginning to cut all hesitation. As we clearly recollect the image of the Ashe, we are purifying, accumulating vast amounts of virtue. As we let the Ashe's meaning permeate our being, we are accumulating vast amounts of Great Eastern Sun wisdom. Virtue and wisdom are coming together in the heart center to establish Shambhala sacred outlook. Now the Ashe rests in the heart center and we can feel its incredible power. We should remember that in our body there is an actual Ashe that has the qualities of everything we're talking about.

Now we are filled with utter confidence that we are being

touched and blessed by the Rigdens. They are—almost with their hands—transplanting our own heart with the Ashe and saying, "Here is your real heart." We feel the Ashe—mercy, brilliance, confidence, egolessness—in our heart center, which is, from a meditation perspective, the source of everything.

Just meditating on those principles, contemplating them, resting in that kind of knowledge and certainty, begins to make the Ashe hum and vibrate. It is sending out awakened signals, cutting thoughts, waking up the rest of the cells in our body, and we begin to experience a sense of energy. Our mind isn't particularly agitated, but it has tremendous warmth. This is the life force of all and the confidence of all. We extend the energy in all directions. Then, without hesitation, we open our eyes, relax our eyes—it's not particularly a staring contest—and feel that now we are the Ashe.

We feel Ashe in the heart and expand out, resting our mind in that nakedness without manipulation. We have awakened the Ashe, the primordial stroke. We're full of primordialness and compassion. This is the dzogrim, or completion stage of our meditation, in which we rest in wisdom. We are resting in Ashe, which is empty of concepts.

As we expand out, we are practicing being free from holding onto a fallacy of who we are. Holding onto who we think we are wears down our mind. Now we can simply let the mind be free of that. We can rest in the naked truth, our field of power, suchness itself. Without the notion of self and its baggage, experiences are simple, free, and nonconceptual. Obviously we are not going to be able to have a complete experience of this state—we may only have glimpses. But once we know what it is, we can try to have them often.

Authentic presence—wangthang—is egoless practice. As we stay here, we feel delight. Because our mind is free of conceptuality and we know how things are, we have a sense of humor. We are experiencing the dralas of awakened mind. We have been given the most precious of jewels—our own awakening, our own understanding of tatagatagharba, sugatagarba, going to bliss.

What does it to mean to go to bliss? The mind is no longer burdened by having to hold onto things in a conceptual or dualistic way. It seems more and more silly to hold on to the illusion of self. As we begin to release that, we have an experience of enjoyment, a sense of complete celebration. In Tibetan we sometimes say *trowa*—delight, joy, being cheerful. These are all more attributes of windhorse.

We also feel fearless. We are no longer afraid of space, no longer afraid of our own mind, no longer afraid of being left alone and bored to death. Since avoiding boredom has been the major hidden agenda for most of our life, our mind is free. We also understand why we were afraid of boredom: we were afraid to discover our own egolessness.

Once we have this kind of understanding, we want to share it with others. Therefore we extend our understanding, mercy, compassion, and insight to all. Seeing that our lungta is not just for ourselves, we offer it because we no longer feel miserly. We are free to offer our realization because we understand the nature of it. In fact, giving it away is a sign of our realization. Therefore we are very courageous and daring, because now we have the confidence, ability, and will to go out and accomplish a greater field of potency and power, a greater authentic presence for the benefit of others. That is the basis of creating an enlightened world.

16

GUIDED MEDITATION: EXECUTING
THE STROKE OF ASHE

IN THE MOVIE "Hero," after the characters do calligraphy, nothing can kill them. They're just ordinary people doing calligraphy, but their confidence gives them power—more power than somebody without confidence who has a gun. That's the power of executing the stroke of Ashe. When the warrior makes a stroke with profound dignity—even with a brush—he or she has ziji.

This brush is not just an ordinary brush; this ink is not ordinary ink. We are empowering it and then using its power. As warriors, we are taking it and saying, "Now I am going to sit on my throne." We're going to take the brush, which will be like a very sharp knife that can cut conceptualization. When we touch the ink to our tongues, that is *damtsik*, samaya, our commitment. Commitment to what? To the Great Eastern Sun, to basic goodness, to acting with compassion. That is our oath and our practice. Most of us need the opportunity to clarify our intention and back it up with an oath. When we make an oath, it stays in our consciousness and becomes the seed for future actions.

With that inspiration we execute the Ashe with brush and ink, which is the acting out of reality. When we draw a mandala, we are acting out the realm of the *herukas* and *dakinis*. If we're doing lama dancing, we are acting out the sacred realm. My relatives do Gesar dances, which originated from visions of Mipham the Great. They involve visualizing and saying certain words. The dakinis say something and the herukas say something, back and forth. These dances increase the lungta and windhorse of the entire region. In the same way, by acting out the Ashe in stroke practice, we are using a particular form to invigorate our lungta.

By taking the brush we are automatically harnessing drala energy. We dip the brush into the ink, not all the way down, stirring it to the right and to the left, feeling the ink, getting the right amount. As we touch the ink to our tongue, we are taking the oath of Shambhala—surrendering our eyes, heart, and tongue to the highest truth. Taking the brush into our mouth and the ink on our tongue symbolizes how seriously we are regarding this practice.

Then we raise the brush and hold it straight out in front of us for a moment. In this movement, we are expressing our mindfulness and awareness, which magnetizes the dralas. The channels in our body become awakened. We are relaxed, but with tremendous confidence. Then we're bringing the brush down, touching the paper, which is a vast expanse. As we do this, we're bringing along the drala energy of the mother lineage, the father lineage, and the imperial lineages. We are enacting the energy of all the lineage beings before us, bringing it into the ink and the paper.

It is said that when each of us is born, the energy of the mother lineage, the father lineage, and also uncle lineages and all kinds of things, is there. Whether we like our relatives or not, we can turn that energy into power. That's why we do lineage chants—because the energy is continuous. If we denigrate our family, we ourselves are weakened. When we respect our lineages, the dralas stay on our shoulders, on our back, on our head. When somebody with good drala goes into battle, even if they're not really big, they look big. Even if they're not all that graceful, they look graceful. That's the impression people get when we have drala energy.

Then we draw to the left, up toward the right, and start cutting down to overcome obstacles. That's the notion of enemy. Obviously the ultimate enemy is klesha, setting sun. So we are cutting through that, but without aggression. Making a stroke represents that kind of wrathful activity. The downward stroke is the notion of subjugating, penetrating, and having a confident nonaggressive way of overcoming obstacles: severe negative emotions such as anger, desire, pride, and jealousy. In the mandala principle these are in the four directions—in the east, anger; in the south, pride; in the west, desire; and in the north, ignorance. There are different correlations in terms of what practice we are doing, but the downward stroke is quelling all those elements. We can also relate to it in terms of quelling any kind of obstacle in our life at that particular time.

The Ashe has the quality of the dagger or *phurba*, which is used to overcome passion, aggression, and ignorance. The whole stroke has the element of beginning—primordialness—as well as the quality of invoking. So first we invoke our own personal drala or energy, and then, as we take the stroke down, we cut whatever obstacles are hindering us. It's important when we're doing it in daily practice to actually visualize that we're overcoming any obstacles we have by using these principles from the Shambhala teachings. After we've finished cutting down, we dedicate our activity to others by wishing that it may inspire all beings, taking the stroke out to the other side. The stroke contains all the elements of our intention: beginning, invoking, cutting, overcoming, and dedicating our activity to others.

Stroke practice is not something we do 100,000 times. It has more to do with quality than quantity. We can do it a few times and get the energy of the practice. It is laying the foundation for the environment, the mandala of dralas. Dralas themselves help us on the path to enlightenment. There has not been a single great being who has attained realization who did not have the complete support of all the dralas.

When I learned how to do calligraphy, I was instructed that I was not just drawing a letter, I was drawing a bodhisattva. In stroke practice, we hold that kind of attitude. One of the Dorje Dradül's inspirations when he came to the West was that even though technology offers us lots of convenience and benefit, to a certain degree modern life has robbed us of our dignity and potency. One purpose of Ashe practice is to rouse those powers. Hopefully doing this kind of practice will enable us to recognize drala, the ability to create magic in our body, mind, and environment. Once we begin to notice the drala in our life, we are more able to see when it isn't there.

In stroke practice, we're developing the ability to have a mind like the slogan under the garuda—"profound, brilliant, just, powerful, and all-victorious." Executing the Ashe as a group has the effect of increasing our ziji exponentially.

This practice was very important to my father. It is one of his seed-syllable teachings. It's unique to our lineage and tradition. It's up to us to hand it on.

17
THE JOURNEY

I BELIEVE that the Dorje Dradül's coming to the West when he did was not accidental, but totally auspicious, timely, and interdependent with what is happening in the world today. Even though he expounded a vast variety of teachings, none seemed dearer to his heart than these teachings on Shambhala. He dressed, walked, and ate according to those principles.

Now there are many of us who have entered the Shambhala path in order to clarify and understand our own mind and heart. Once we've established some kind of clarity and strength, what can we do? We can begin to look at the world around us and realize the suffering, the confusion, and the aggression. Managing these situations is a challenge, but as Shambhala warriors we know them as the barbarians we are inspired to overcome.

We are in a unique situation in that we have this practice of Ashe, which is a personal practice of gaining confidence and strength in order to come out of hiding. Because of the extreme pressures of the world, we've figured out some very clever and systematic ways to buffer ourselves from the environment. In training as warriors, we cultivate the courage to emerge from those patterns. Once we come out, what do we see? We see the nature of human society and we automatically have compassion. We also have great love. The warrior has love. That is what is burning, our desire to actually help sentient beings—not our desire to make a better toaster.

We need to realize that this desire to help others is the heart's blood of what we are doing. Although it is easily accessible, it is not easily developed. The mind we are developing with Ashe is complete confidence, where one has gone from earth into heaven and now can join the two. Binding heaven and earth is the activity of a Sakyong or a Sakyong Wangmo, which is what we become when we do it. The strength of this particular approach depends on clarifying the Ashe. A is the primordial nature. She is the stroke that cuts at all times the individual who is trying to denigrate the situation. The more we clarify the Ashe, the more confidence we have.

What we call Shambhala is a union of many different traditions' wisdom and knowledge, all for the purposes of uplifting our physical environment, applying discipline or exertion to our body, or developing mindfulness and awareness of mind. But what makes our tradition Shambhala is the mind treasure of the Dorje Dradül, encapsulated in the primordial stroke of Ashe.

THE SAKYONG

The Sakyong is the protector in the center of Shambhala vision, inspiring people to participate and to create enlightened mandala. The word *sakyong* literally means "earth protector"; the Sakyong protects the mind's ground nature—basic goodness—from confusion and doubt. The Sakyong is also a teacher who comments upon and holds the Shambhala terma teachings and practices. Dedication to the Sakyong is dedication to creating a better world. Our practice is to see these two commitments as inseparable and equally part of the path.

My understanding is that as the Sakyong I have a direct relationship with the people. By nature I'm asked to fill a particular post based on the bodhisattva vow of helping people. It fulfills the need of the people to be led, helped, and supported in some way. The tradition we have is democratic in that every individual has the possibility to achieve complete enlightenment. In that sense no one is higher or lower than anyone else.

With that possibility comes individual responsibility. The Sakyong holds the individual to certain values, but we are responsible for our own conduct. The Sakyong is an example demonstrating to people that they have to rise up and participate. Creating a society takes exertion. It takes all of us working together. We have a community and there are problems, there are issues. Calling ourselves Shambhalians, Buddhists, or a sangha does not make us perfect. But by coming together we are acknowledging the fact that we would like to move together in a forward direction of betterment. What does betterment mean? It means getting involved in the process of developing a community. Community implies work—I don't know how else to say it. It takes work to live together. Work means sacrifice and discipline, and it also means love.

Learning how to be in a community is ultimately what we are talking about in terms of enlightened society. It means that individuals are not wallowing in their own kleshic juices. Instead, we are developing the strength of mind—having tiger, lion, garuda, dragon vision—to rise up and say, "I do not have to solve problems with hatred or jealousy; I have other tools, such as raising windhorse and moving forward with confidence. This time I'm going to use these instead."

We're using big words here—"enlightened society"—for a very basic choice. Rising beyond aggression is how we bring together our inspiration and vision so that Shambhala is everywhere. We have to work in this way. That's what I mean by balance. I will certainly do what I can. However, as I've said before, this is not for me, it's for you. In fact, we could each have that attitude: "It is not particularly for me, it's for everybody else." The point is to look at what is going on, take personal responsibility for it, and ask, "How can I help?"

DISCOVERING SHAMBHALA IN OUR MIND STREAM

Most of us think of the mind as very solid. It appears to be very solid. Looking around, we can see that we have literally divided up the world with our projections. Everywhere we look there are little hooks of aggression and desire. We cannot scan the room without having four or five major opinions.

This is just hooking. When we find ourselves doing it, we can ask, "Is this really necessary?"

I'm not talking about trying to abstain from visual contact. To liberate our mind we need to realize that it is not "me" looking around the room with my eyes. We need to have confidence in the relative Ashe and let our eyes just be. That way we can see things for what they really are. What naturally arises from that confidence are the elements of meek, perky, outrageous, and inscrutable, which emerge from the continuum of our mind. That is Shambhala on a very personal level. The golden age of Shambhala comes from our being able to discover it in our mind stream.

Physiologically speaking, our mind gravitates toward a center around this particular body, so there is a direct relationship with the Ashe going on. This is an inner yoga practice; we are relating with the core of our physical situation. When we rise from our morning practice, we go out into the world where everybody is putting their hands all over everything. We look and see that all this hooking makes everybody really upset. Why do people do it? We do it because we are all fearful, and therefore all our senses are like jackals and hyenas continually jumping up and down, to echo the words of the *Sadhana of Mahamudra*. Our perceptions are like scavengers looking for bits of confirmation everywhere.

In Shambhala we talk about liberating those perceptions. Let them be garuda, with no bounds. It is a self-reflective meditation, looking at our state of mind until the moment when we say, "I can do this right now." Then instantly we are born into the family of Shambhala. We have gotten our passport and we are ready to travel.

I hope we can all join together in taking this journey. We are starting with the principles of enlightenment, decency, and dignity for every individual. Ultimately that is true democracy. From that point of view every individual is the Rigden king, the unfathomable mind of complete confidence. One day—tonight, tomorrow, or in a few lifetimes—we will all realize our enlightenment. We will wake up and the world will appear unfettered and luminous, completely rich and clear. What brings about that moment? The only difference between that moment and any other is our confidence, pure and real.

Editor's Note

AS ASHE is a unique and pivotal practice within the Shambhala community, it has been my delight to compile the Sakyong's teachings on this practice for students at the Warrior Assembly level and beyond.

The content of this book is drawn mainly from the transcripts of the 2000 and 2003 Kalapa Assemblies. The stroke and wind-horse transmissions are taken from the 2005 and 2007 Vajrayana Seminaries. Also included are the Sakyong's remarks to a Warrior Assembly at Shambhala Mountain Center in 2007.

The following people were helpful in bringing this book to publication: Acharya Eve Rosenthal; transcribers Edith Sage, Kristine McCutcheon, and others; copyeditor Alice Haspray; designer Chris Gibson; proofreader John Sell; and translator Scott Wellenbach. At Shambhala Media, Terry Rudderham, Gordon Kidd, Chris Levy, and Kiersten Gaetz have provided steady encouragement, as has David Brown of the Office of the Sakyong.

Most of all, I am deeply grateful to the Sakyong for elaborating on the Dorje Dradül's profound legacy of Ashe. I am honored to work with him. May his teachings continue to inspire Shambhalians everywhere, bringing benefit to all.

KI KI SO SO
Emily Hilburn Sell
Halifax
April 2009

GLOSSARY

ABHISHEKA Tib. *wang* [dbang] Empowerment, sprinkling.

AMRITA Tib. *dütsi* [bdud rtsi] Intoxicant.

ASHE [aa sha] Primordial stroke.

BODHICHITTA Tib. *changchup kyi sem* [byang chub kyi sems] On the relative level, this is the wish to attain buddhahood for the sake of all sentient beings, together with the practice necessary to accomplish this. On the absolute level, it is nondual wisdom, the ultimate nature of the mind and the true status of all phenomena.

BODHISATTVA Tib. *changchup sempa* [byang chub sems dpa'] Lit. "enlightenment being."

CHÖGYAL [chos rgyal] Dharma king.

CHÖYING [chos dbyings] Skt. *dharmadhatu* Sphere of reality, realm of dharma, active space.

DAKINI Tib. *khandro* [mkha' 'dro ma] Lit. "moving through space." The representation of wisdom in female form.

DAMTSIK [dam tshig] Skt. *samaya* Binding vow, commitment, words of honor.

DAPÖN [mda' dpon] General.

DÖMA-NE SANGPO [gdod ma nas bzang po] Basic or primordial goodness.

DORJE DRADÜL [rdo rje dgra 'dul] Indestructible warrior; lit. "indestructible tamer of enemies."

DRALA [dgra bla *or* dgra lha] Lit. "above the enemy," those who conquer aggression.

DZOKCHEN [rdzogs chen] Great completion. Also known as great perfection and ati yoga, the highest teachings of the nine-yana path.

DZOGRIM [rdzogs rim] Skt. *sampannakrama* Completion, perfection stage or practice. One of the two stages of sadhana practice, in which the practitioner dissolves the visualization and meditates formlessly. This breaks any fixation that may have developed from the visualization. The defining practice of the nontheistic approach.

GEWA [dge ba] Virtue.

HERUKA Tib. *trakthung* [khrag 'thung] A wrathful male yidam, the masculine principle of energy and skillful means.

KAMA [bka' ma] Teachings that are not terma, teachings received from a teacher.

KHORWA ['khor ba] Skt. *samsara* Cyclic existence; it arises out of ignorance and is characterized by suffering.

KLESHA Tib. *nyönmong* [nyon mongs] Affliction, poisonous emotion.

KYERIM [bskyed rim] Skt. *utpattikrama* Developmental or generation stage. One of the two stages of sadhana practice, in which the practitioner develops and meditates with a visualization. This stage has an emphasis on form.

LHA [lha] Deity.

LHASANG [lha bsangs] Ceremony in which juniper is offered in order to bringing down blessings.

LHÜNDRUP [lhun grub] Spontaneous presence, spontaneously, naturally.

LUNG [rlung] Skt. *prana* Wind, life force.

LUNGTA [rlung rta] Windhorse.

MAHAMUDRA Tib. *chakchen* [phyag chen], abbreviated form of *chakgya chenpo* [phyag rgya chen po] Great symbol.

MANDALA Tib. *kyilkhor* [dkyil 'khor] Lit. "center–fringe."

MIGEWA [mi dge ba] Nonvirtue.

PADMASAMBHAVA "The lotus-born." Venerated as "Guru Rinpoche," he brought Buddhism to Tibet.

PAKCHAK [bag chags] Habitual tendencies.

PAYU [pha yul] Discernment.

PHURBA [phur ba] Skt. *kila* Ritual dagger.

PRAJNA Tib. *sherab* [shes rab] Best knowledge.

RIGDEN [rigs ldan] Holder of the family, monarch of Shambhala.

SAB SEL SONG TSEN KÜNTU GYAL [zab gsal srong btsan kun tu rgyal] Profound, brilliant, just, powerful, all-victorious.

SAKYONG [sa skyong] Earth protector.

SAKYONG WANGMO [sa skyong dbang mo] Earth protector queen.

SAMSARA Tib. *khorwa* ['khor ba] Circular. The vicious cycle of transmigratory existence.

SEM [sems] Mundane mind.

SEM-LE DEPA [sems las 'das pa] Beyond conventional mind.

SHAMATHA Tib. *shi-ne* [zhi gnas] Peacefully abiding, dwelling in peace or tranquility.

SHARCHEN NYIMA [shar chen nyi ma] Great Eastern Sun.

SHIWA ÖKAR [zhi ba 'od dkar] Lit. "peaceful white light."

SÖNAM [bsod nams] Merit.

SOY-YIK [srog yig] Seed syllable.

SUGATAGARBHA Tib. *dewar shek-pe nyingpo* [bde bar gshegs pa'i snying po] The heart or essence of going into bliss or joy.

TATHAGATAGARBHA Tib. *teshek nyingpo* [de gshegs snying po] Buddha nature.

TATHATA Tib. *te-shin-nyi* [de bzhin nyid] Suchness, things as they are, the world as seen from sacred outlook.

TERMA [gter ma] Treasure, hidden teachings revealed.

TERTÖN [gter ston] Someone who receives terma.

THIN-LE [phrin las] Buddha activity.

TIMUK [gti mug] Bewilderment.

TRISONG DETSEN An eighth-century Tibetan dharma king who played a pivotal role in the introduction of Buddhism to Tibet and the establishment of the Nyingma, or "ancient" school of Tibetan Buddhism.

TROWA [spro ba] Cheerful, joyful.

TSE-CHIK [rtse gcig] One-pointed.

UPAYA Tib. *thap* [thabs] Method, skillful means.

VAJRASATTVA Tib. *Dorje Sempa* [rdo rje sems pa] "Indestructible pure being." Vajrasattva embodies the principle of purity and purification.

VIPASHYANA Tib. *lhakthong* [lhag mthong] Clear seeing, superior insight, higher view.

WANGTHANG [dbang thang] Authentic presence.

WERMA [wer ma] A class of Tibetan deities, sometimes said to be the messengers of the drala.

YE-NE [ye nas] Primordially pure.

YESHE [ye shes] Wisdom.

YÖNTEN [yon tan] Virtuous enlightened qualities.

YÜN [dbyun] Energy spot.

ZIJI [gzi brjid] Confidence, shining out.